Nearly 2,000 years ago a man named Jesus walked the long road from the treacherously beautiful Garden of Gethsemane to his own Crucifixion on Calvary.

He was betrayed by those he trusted, denied by his friends, mistried by false priests and abandoned by a politician who, although sympathetic, chose "neutrality" over involvement and changed the course of mankind.

Yet Jesus overcame his most trying hour, and in his trial—and his triumph—is God's greatest legacy to all men everywhere, for all time.

AT THE CROSS tells the 2,000-year-old story that offers ever-new meaning for all who will allow themselves to experience it.

D1413918

AT THE CROSS

CHARLES LUDWIG

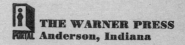

THE WARNER PRESS
Anderson, Indiana

AT THE CROSS

A PORTAL BOOK
Published by Pyramid Publications for Warner Press, Inc.

Portal edition published November, 1974

Copyright ©, 1961, by Warner Press, Inc. Copyright ©,
1974 (Revised Edition), by Warner Press, Inc.
All Rights Reserved

ISBN: 0-87162-178-9

Printed in the United States of America

PORTAL BOOKS are published by Warner Press, Inc.
1200 East 5th Street, Anderson, Indiana 46011, U.S.A.

CONTENTS

AT THE CROSS

Foreword by
DR. FRANK C. LAUBACH

To have read this beautiful interpretation of the Cross is one of the rich experiences of my life, and thousands will live more patiently, love more tenderly, speak more softly, and suffer more courageously because they have walked with Charles Ludwig from Gethsemane to Calvary.

The Cross is a very timely theme in this day when we tremble at the edge of catastrophe.

But this book is more than emotion and inspiration. It sparkles with fresh information and insights which not one person in a million would gather elsewhere. What a wealth of material for sermons and for Sunday school teachers!

This book has succeeded better than any other I have read in linking the Gethsemane of Jesus with our own. There Jesus "fought the greatest battle of all time" and yet it is a battle we all face sooner or later. Many will go through the valley more courageously if they read this vivid story of how Jesus sought an escape which he could not have and rose triumphantly to face his fearful ordeal.

The chapters on "The Arrest," "Before Caiaphas," "Pilate's Basin," "Simon of Cyrene," "At the Cross" are all magnificently terrible. When you finish each one, you feel as though your very soul has been bathed in the blood of Christ and has come out clean.

Charles Ludwig is a brilliant minister, raised on an African mission field, who loves his Lord so dearly he went to the scene of earth's greatest tragedy in Jerusalem and followed Jesus from Gethsemane to the Cross of Calvary. The result is this story, full of passion, love, and power.

New York, 1961

This introduction was written for the first edition of this book. Since then, the book has been thoroughly revised and slightly enlarged.

CHAPTER I

GETHSEMANE!

And they came to a place which was named Gethsemane: and he saith to his disciples, Sit ye here, while I shall pray.

And he taketh with him Peter and James and John, and began to be sore amazed, and to be very heavy;

And saith unto them, My soul is exceeding sorrowful unto death: tarry ye here, and watch.

And he went forward a little, and fell on the ground, and prayed that, if it were possible, the hour might pass from him (Mark 14:32-35).

Time has a way of inflating money and eroding words. It distorts them—gives them new meaning. Thus, because the Hospital of Bethlehem in London was an insane asylum, the lovely word *Bethlehem* skidded into the horrible word *bedlam*.

Alas, the expression *Gethsemane* is suffering the same fate! It still refers to the Garden on the slopes of the Mount of Olives where Jesus agonized before God. But the word is beginning to mean *a crisis that should be avoided*.

Indeed, some are proclaiming that we should have a crown without a cross!

A visitor to Bible Lands is generally a little disappointed as he visits the spots made famous by the birth, ministry, death, and resurrection of Jesus Christ. A reason for this disappointment is that

9

shrines have been built over many of the traditional places, making it difficult to imagine the scene just as it was when Jesus was there in the flesh.

At the end of the narrow road that leads in winding curves up to Bethlehem one does not see an ancient stable where an anxious Joseph and Mary heard Jesus' first cries; instead, he sees an elaborate building known as the Church of the Nativity.

Here one is told that the pillars of the building were salvaged from the Temple in Jerusalem by the order of Queen Helena. And the guide points out an elaborate altar covered with gold and silver candlesticks which he declares are lit perpetually. Then with a hushed voice and in his best professional manner he calls attention to a large silver star imbedded in the floor and exclaims, "That is the exact spot where Christ was born!"

At the end of the Via Dolorosa, over which Jesus swayed and staggered some twenty centuries ago with a heavy cross over his shoulders, the visitor is again confronted with a large building—the Church of the Holy Sepulchre.[1] This elaborate structure is a vast jungle of gold, silver, polished marble, flickering candles, breath-taking chandeliers, and elaborate mosaics. No expense was spared to make the place lovely, inspiring, unforgettable.

But again one is disappointed by all this gold, silver, and marble. It just does not blend in with one's idea of the old rugged Cross and Easter morning. Most of us would prefer the place to be just as it was when the Cross became crimson with the lifeblood of the One who died for our sins. Indeed, it would be a wonderful thing if all the shrines could be removed. Their removal would make the historic

[1] This building was started in A.D. 325 by the order of Constantine. It is thought by many that the building surrounds Calvary and the tomb of Christ. Others dispute this, declaring that Gordon's Calvary, discovered in the nineteenth century by General "Chinese" Gordon, to be the actual place.

sites much more authentic, and the salvaged gold and silver would support an army of missionaries!

There are, however, several uncontaminated places in this land of Jesus. And one of these is the truly exquisite Garden of Gethsemane. There you will not find man-made walls, red-tiled roofs, polished marble, and hammered gold.

This hallowed spot with its eight ancient olive trees is now tended by Franciscan friars. These men can be seen almost any day as, dressed in their long brown habits and armed with rakes, they work in the garden keeping it immaculate.

These kindly men have a job the tense, high-strung men of our day might well envy.

After one has meditated and prayed in the shadow of one of these gnarled trees—some believe they date back to the Middle Ages, and some imaginative souls even believe that their history extends back to the days of Jesus—he asks himself why the Garden was not ruined by shrines like so many of the other places.

According to tradition, Gethsemane was identified by the chief shrine-maker, Queen Helena, the mother of Constantine, in A.D. 326. Why did she not cover it with a large building? It could have been done easily. And the answer is not because of the lack of money, for she had the vast treasury of the Roman Empire behind her!

Certainly there are many logical answers to this question. But I am going to take the liberty of setting forth the answer that satisfies me. The Church of the Nativity was built over the stable where the Virgin Mary gave birth to Jesus. This virgin birth of Christ is a fact that causes us to rejoice. That a God-man was born, moves us. It stirs us. It puts a song on our lips. And it causes us to bow our heads in worship. But this is an experience with which none of us can readily identify, for no one else was ever born of a virgin—and no one else ever will be. We acknowledge it and are grateful. *But we cannot share it!* We can only know about it from afar.

The Church of the Holy Sepulchre was built, many think, over Calvary. The Cross means everything to those who follow him. With tear-dimmed eyes we sing "The Old Rugged Cross," "Beneath the Cross of Jesus," and "When I Survey the Wondrous Cross." But again, we cannot identify with the Cross, for it is quite unlikely that any of us will ever be crucified. We love the Cross. We bow at the foot of the Cross. The greatest saints, however, even including John and Mary the mother of Jesus, have not felt the darkest moments of the Cross!

Yes, I know library shelves are filled with the histories of Christians who were slowly burned at the stake, pulled apart on the rack, or tortured to death in a thousand other ways. But none of them was carrying the sins of the world! And, moreover, none of them ever cried out in anguish as did Jesus: "My God, My God, why have You abandoned Me—leaving Me helpless, forsaking and failing Me and My Need?" (Matt. 27:46, Amplified).

God never forsakes his own. But here, for a brief moment, Jesus Christ was the emblem of sin, and God can have nothing to do with sin. Hence, the cry.[2]

The Cross—even to the most mystical and spiritual saint—can only be seen in dim outline. We can understand it sufficiently to be saved. But that is all! The total meaning of the Cross is completely beyond the human mind.

But identifying with Jesus in Gethsemane is something else, even though that identification is extremely small and inadequate. This is so because more people than most of us would think have had

[2] Many seek to limit the impact of these words by pointing out that Jesus was quoting Psalm 22:1.

their knees soiled on the damp grass of a minor Gethsemane. The tattered register of "Heartbreak Hotel" is filled—and overflowing.

At Gethsemane, Queen Helena undoubtedly had more real identification than at any of the other sacred spots. Although her beginnings are obscure, it is quite certain that she was born in poverty—perhaps even slavery. It is also claimed that she had been a barmaid. Then she either married or was the concubine of Emperor Constantius Chlorus.

But being the first lady in the Roman Empire did not last, for soon Constantius put her away for political reasons and married Theodora.

These events must have torn at her soul! Indeed, it was this pain and the influence of her only son, Constantine, that turned her to Christ.

With this background, Queen Helena's eyes must have filled many a time as she walked through the Garden of Gethsemane. Here, her identification was too complete. Thus, she did not build a shrine over the place. The little garden was just too sacred for that! The place came within her personal experience!

Where your Gethsemane is, I do not know. It may be at a classroom desk, behind a pulpit, on the mission field, in a prison cell, in front of a sink piled high with dishes, in a wheelchair, or between the white sheets of a hospital bed.

There is no way for me to know where your place of testing is. But I do know that if you are a sincere Christian you will have such a place sooner or later. Nevertheless, I must say from my own personal experience and personal observation and from my reading and understanding of the Scriptures that it is a distinct privilege to enter and have a real Gethsemane!

But before we consider *your* Gethsemane, where you wrestle with your temptation, and where your heart nearly breaks, we must consider the one that was faced by our elder brother, Jesus Christ!

In the quietness of the Upper Room Jesus had girded himself with a towel and washed the disciples' feet. He had had the Last Supper and instituted communion. He had seen the face of Judas harden and had watched him sneak out into the night. Then, after they had sung a hymn (the Hallel), he led the eleven down the stone steps and out onto the ancient streets of Jerusalem. A full paschal moon lighted the skies, and there was the sound of multitudes of pilgrims as they gathered into the Holy City for the Passover.[3]

Jesus led his followers by the lower pool and out through the Fountain Gate. Then he turned left and followed a path that hugged the walls of the city. At last the Temple came into view. Solomon's porch was brilliantly lighted. They could see the huge, golden grapevine that adorned the massive gates. It was perhaps in this area that Jesus stopped and gave them a parable. John has recorded it for us in the Gospel that bears his name: "I am the vine, ye are the branches: He that abideth in me, and I in him, the same bringeth forth much fruit: for without me ye can do nothing" (John 15:5).

After finishing the parable, Christ applied it so that it could be completely understood, and then he and his disciples continued on their journey. They passed the historic tomb of Absalom, crossed the stone bridge that arched the brook Kidron, and trudged on until they came to the Garden of Gethsemane. Here Jesus stopped and asked eight of his disciples to wait on the outside. Then he took Peter, James, and John, and entered the place where he was to fight the greatest battle of all time.

[3] Normally Jerusalem had a population of 150,000 to 200,000. But as many as 3,000,000 attended Passover.

At this point the readers of the event must wonder what those eight men had to say about being left outside. Did they complain? We will never know!

But among those who were not invited into Gethsemane was Thomas. Thomas was a faithful disciple. When the others of the Twelve were afraid to go into Judea for fear of the Jews, he spoke up at once. "Let us also go, that we may die with him" (John 11:16). Bold words. Still he was not invited into the Garden.

Nathaniel was a proven disciple. His record is clear. When Jesus saw him, he exclaimed, "Behold an Israelite indeed, in whom is no guile!" But Jesus did not extend an invitation to him to enter the sacred place.

Those eight men on the outside loved Jesus. And yet, for one reason or another, Jesus did not feel that they were quite ready for Gethsemane.

Yes, it is a privilege to enter Gethsemane!

Peter, James, and John were allowed to enter. But even though they had been present at the Transfiguration, the raising of Jairus' daughter, and many other sacred experiences, Jesus did not allow them to go as far into the Garden as he went!

Oh, you with the broken heart! Oh, you with the vicious temptations! Oh, you with apparently unanswered prayers! Oh, you with agony of soul! You are fortunate, blessed, privileged! The depths of Gethsemane can only be entered by God's choice saints!

This is so because those who enter Gethsemane have to be trusted souls. The salvation of everyone who had ever lived or who will ever live depends on the death of the Lord Jesus Christ.

But God, knowing this and believing in Jesus, took risks with that salvation. Suppose Jesus had yielded to temptation in the wilderness. Or let us suppose he had yielded in Gethsemane. Such thoughts make one dizzy! Had he yielded, there would be no salvation for anyone. No, not even for one!

Jesus, however, did not yield.

Now in the Kingdom there are certain things that no one—I mean absolutely no one—can do as well as you. Thus, if you falter and fail in your Gethsemane, there are certain things that just will not be done.

Imagine, then, the faith that God has in you to allow you to go through an avenue of severe trial. Instead of complaining about your trail of tears, you should thank God for the confidence he has in you. He knows that you can improve through the refining fire. And because he believes in you, he is willing to take certain risks!

Those who have the unique opportunity of being trusted with great suffering, great temptation, and great sorrows have a unique pulpit from which to preach—a pulpit that even death cannot silence.

But someone may say, "All of this sounds very Pollyannaish and heroic. Nevertheless, there is no cheer for me. My Gethsemane is much too bitter for that. I don't think I can stand it any more. The arthritis is too twisting; the pain is too severe; the enemy is much too close. I think I'll be forced to give up."

Yes, there are bitter Gethsemanes through which many Christians are privileged to pass. Some are so bitter they cause the imagination to reel. Even so, Jesus led the way through every type of sorrow, and he will lead us and support us when the going is so rough we are about to break. Remember we have a promise, "There hath no temptation taken you but such as is common to man: but God is faithful, who will not suffer you to be tempted above that ye are able; but will with the temptation also make a way to escape, that ye may be able to bear it" (1 Cor. 10:13).

Sometimes, however, it seems that he knows how

much we can bear right down to the last broken straw. Nevertheless—!

But before you maximize your dark hour, it might be well to consider the bitterness which Jesus faced on that trying Thursday night. Let's look at the account as recorded in Mark 14:33-36 and translated by J.B. Phillips:

"He took with him Peter, James and John, and began to be horror-stricken and desperately depressed.

"'My heart is nearly breaking,' he told them. 'Stay here and watch for me.'

"Then he walked forward a little way and flung himself on the ground, praying that, if it were possible, he might not have to face the ordeal.

"'Dear Father,' he said, 'all things are possible to you. Please—let me not have to drink this cup! Yet it is not what I want but what you want.'"

When we remember that these words were the words of the Son of God who helped form the planets, who is clothed with glory and honor, who knew no sin, and who was from the beginning, we know it was a bitter experience indeed.

Another point to remember is that most of us find ourselves suddenly thrust into a Gethsemane. All at once, without warning, and without the suffering of anticipation, the day of decision and struggle is upon us.

But this was not true with Jesus Christ. As "the Lamb slain from the foundation of the world" (Rev. 13:8), he felt the agony of Gethsemane and Calvary from the very beginning. When iron was first formed in the mountains and valleys he knew that one day bits of it would be fashioned into square-headed nails that would be smashed through his hands and feet, and he suffered.

When trees began to grow, he knew that one day a tree would be fashioned into a cross on which he would be suspended, and he suffered. And when thorns began to grow in the harsh land of Judea, he knew that one day a crown would be made of them and that crown would be placed on his head and wantonly pounded into his flesh. And he suffered.

That night when Jesus crossed the brook Kidron, he crossed it at the place where his royal ancestor David had crossed it nearly one thousand years before. On that occasion David was barefoot and in sackcloth, and was fleeing from his son Absalom. King David's heart was broken. It was almost more than he could bear.

But the suffering of Jesus in Gethsemane was infinitely more intense than that of the former king; for piled upon Jesus were all the sins of David, all the sins of Absalom, all the sins of the ancient world, all the sins of the Dark Ages, all the sins of the modern world, and all the sins of the ages to come.

Jesus Christ who loathed sin, and who never sinned, was to become sin for us. Or, as Paul expressed it to the Corinthians, "For he hath made him to be sin for us, who knew no sin; that we might be made the righteousness of God in him" (2 Cor. 5:21).

But now let us get a picture of Jesus in the Garden. We see him at the rocklike base of an olive tree. The moon is shining through the leaves lighting up his face. His face is creased with deep lines of anxiety, pain, and care. For a while he prays on his knees. Then, in convulsive agony, he flings his whole body on the ground. The smell of burning grapevines and rancid olive oil drifts through the air. Nearby a huge circular stone stands on end in the hollow of even a larger stone. The upper stone is pierced by a long pole, and this pole is the means for turning the upper stone and thus crushing the olives.

This olive press is quite symbolic, for Jesus is about to be ruthlessly crushed. Even now, Judas is at the Temple gathering the rabble who will sneeringly turn the stone and squeeze the life out of this eldest son of Mary.

Peter, James, and John—their heads on the roots of an olive tree about one hundred feet away —are at rest. To the left Christ can see the dancing flames of light from Solomon's porch, and on either side he can see the lights in the homes of those preparing for Passover.

All at once the Roman bugle sounds. It is the signal for the change of the watch in the Tower of Antonia. Then the three weary disciples hear the voice of Jesus coming through the crisp morning air as he prays, "Abba, Father, all things are possible unto thee; take away this cup from me: nevertheless not what I will, but what thou wilt" (Mark 14:36).

The Master continues in prayer. But Peter, James, and John just cannot keep their eyes open. It has been a long day. They have been up since early morning. Jesus has taught them many things and their bodies are tired from learning. Soon their eyes close again and they slide into heavy sleep.

But in a moment Jesus is shaking them awake. He rebukes them mildly, and says to Peter, "Sleepest thou? couldest not thou watch one hour?" (v. 37).

Jesus then returns to his place of prayer—still out of bounds for the three disciples—and starts with his previous supplication. There is a sob in his voice. He sounds much as he sounded when he prayed at the tomb of Lazarus. Only this time there is no apparent result.

One would think that through this prayer the whole situation would have changed—that Jesus would be allowed to escape the Cross. After all, he is the only begotten Son. He is without sin. He has been obedient. His prayers had healed lepers; fed multitudes, raised the dead, calmed the sea, healed the blind, and opened the ears of the deaf.

But this time his prayers did not seem to be answered. It seemed that they were in vain!

After agonizing for a long time, Jesus returned to the three disciples and again found them asleep. Again, he shook them awake and then returned to his chosen place and repeated his prayer. And this time, according to Luke, his agony was so great that "there appeared unto him an angel from heaven, strengthening him. And being in an agony he prayed more earnestly: and his sweat was as it were great drops of blood falling down to the ground" (Luke 22:43-44).

This incident in Gethsemane is a lesson for us, preached by Jesus with his actions. Often when we feel that our prayers are getting through, that we are having a response, the experience becomes to the soul what marching feet, beating drums and waving flags are to the spirit. But how do we act when we do not get our way—when our prayers seem to bounce back, unheard and unheeded?

The Master has a lesson for us here! We dare not miss it! Part of the chorus of the song "Wonderful Power in Prayer" by Eliza E. Hewitt goes like this:

For it moveth the Arm that moveth the worlds,
There's a wonderful pow'r in prayer.

It is very true that God's arm has been moved and that it will be moved again and again. Abraham moved it. Moses moved it. Jesus moved it. Paul moved it. And we can move it. Our greatest moments of victory, however, are not when we move God, *but when he moves us!*

God's will was not changed at Gethsemane even though he was addressed most earnestly by his own dear Son. Nevertheless, God sent an angel to strengthen him, and he listened to his prayers. But he did not agree that Jesus should escape the Cross! And because Jesus was obedient and prayed "thy will be done," we have salvation.

Thank God for Christ's obedience!

Would it not be a wonderful thing if we would exercise more effort trying to fit into God's plans rather than trying to get him to fit into our neat little schemes? Of course it is true that Jesus taught us to pray with importunity. We have his sublime parable of the woman and the judge. And there are times when we should pray like this. Nevertheless we should long for the fulfillment of his will—not ours.

If in the Garden of Gethsemane Jesus had prayed, "Father, I insist! I must have my way," he could have, as he reminded Peter at the time of his arrest, asked and received more than twelve legions of angels to deliver him. That would have meant seventy-two thousand of the heavenly host, and there is no doubt but what they could have delivered him and destroyed his enemies. But had Jesus prayed such a prayer, there would be no example of a great victory in a difficult Gethsemane.

No one should be afraid of the will of God. It is always—without exception—for our best and his best interests!

Chapter II

THE ARREST

And as soon as he was come, he goeth straight-way to him, and saith, Master, master; and kissed him.—Mark 14:45-46.

As Jesus sobbed out his last prayer to the Father in Gethsemane, there was almost complete quiet, for it was early in the morning—perhaps 3:00 A.M. The various sounds of the Holy City—people getting ready for the Passover feast, latecomers entering through the Golden Gate, and the bleat of animals near the Temple—had all quieted to near silence.

Everything was quiet except for the gentle rustle of the wind in the olive trees, the occasional barking of a stray dog, and the rhythmic breathing of Peter, James, and John as they slumbered peacefully nearby. And yet in that stillness, in that terrible stillness, in that awful stillness could be heard the prayer of Jesus Christ, the Son of God, as he wrestled with his soul.

Although nearly twenty centuries have rumbled by since that hour of agony, mankind can never forget the words of Jesus' prayer: "Abba, Father, all things are possible unto thee; take away this cup from me: nevertheless not what I will, but what thou wilt" (Mark 14:36).

Then all at once as he pleaded with the Father in that crisp morning air, there was the sound of shuffling feet, snapping twigs, the murmur of voices, and the clang of swords and metal shields.

Jesus turned his face and looked out over the brook Kidron toward the lights of the Temple. But the Temple lights were not the lights that caught his attention, for coming up the slopes of the Mount of Olives was a large gang of men with swinging lanterns and hissing torches. As he watched the intent, sinister mob approach, he could see that it was made up of Temple guards, Roman soldiers, servants of the High Priest, scribes, Pharisees, and even members of the Sanhedrin. Treasurer Judas Iscariot was leading the group.

The Temple guards were unarmed, but the Roman soldiers in their dull-bright helmets were equipped with heavy clubs and keenly sharpened swords. Jesus watched them for a moment, and then he went over to Peter, James, and John. After shaking them awake, he said, "Rise up, let us go; lo, he that betrayeth me is at hand" (Mark 14:42).

In a moment Judas and his followers stepped into the Garden, their lanterns and torches held high. Jesus then stepped into the eerie circle of their lights and said to them, "Whom seek ye?"[1]

The answer came at once, "Jesus of Nazareth."

"I am he," he answered calmly, and I think a thin, friendly smile must have played on his lips.

When he said, "I am he," the crowd moved backward as if pushed by an unseen hand. The men fell clumsily to the ground. Jesus' lofty majesty, purity, humility, kindness, and power was just too much for them!

Jesus then repeated his question, "Whom seek ye?" and in reply, the mob scrambled to its feet and answered, "Jesus of Nazareth."

By this time the eight disciples who had remained on the outside of the Garden had shaken

[1] See John 18: 4-8; Mark 14; Matthew 26; and Luke 22 for this episode.

the sleep out of their eyes and had joined the other three.

"I have told you that I am he," replied Jesus patiently, "if therefore ye seek me, let these go their way."

It was then that Judas stepped out of the shadows. He threw his arms around Jesus and, taking care that the thirty pieces of silver in his pocket didn't jingle, kissed him while he said, "Master, Master."

But now let us borrow the eyes of Simon Peter and view the scene as he must have seen it. Because of the full moon we can see many a detail. The hardened face of the treasurer Judas is a strange contrast of anxiety, cruelty, bewilderment, respect, regret, disappointment, and hatred. The face of Jesus, on the other hand, is much different from what it was an hour ago. Luke pictured him for us as he looked earlier, "And being in an agony he prayed more earnestly: and his sweat was as it were great drops of blood falling down to the ground" (Luke 22:44). Being a doctor, he was impressed with this detail.

Now, however, as we search the face of the Master, we do not see shadows of despair, anxiety, or anger. Instead, we see serenity, triumph, compassion, love. How did this happen? Jesus had won his battle *before* the trial, and thus there is no need for him to battle *during* the trial!

Suddenly we notice that Jesus is focusing his attention on Judas. "Judas," he says, "Judas, betrayest thou the Son of man with a kiss?" (Luke 22:48).

All at once some of the disciples remember that Jesus once said, ". . . and he that hath no sword, let him sell his garment, and buy one" (22:36). And so one of them says, "Lord, shall we smite with the sword?" (22:49).

But before Jesus can answer, Peter whips a blade from its scabbard and slashes at Malchus, the ser-

vant of the high priest. No doubt he had intended
to split the man's head in two. But being a sailor instead of a solider, he merely cut off his ear!

Poor Peter! He is always doing that which he is
not supposed to do, and not doing that which he
should do. He was told not to sleep, but he slept.
He was told to use kindness, but he resorted to a
sword.

But in a moment, perhaps even before the blood
can stream down the neck of Malchus, Jesus
touches the wound; and the ear is as good as new.
The Master now faces Peter and says, "Put up
again thy sword into his place: for all they that
take the sword shall perish with the sword" (Matt.
26:52).

Now the mob starts to bind Jesus with ropes.
They tie his wrists together and pull them up between his shoulder blades according to Roman custom. Next, they put a rope around his neck and
lead him away as if he were a lamb on the way to
slaughter.

The pain of the rope was the first physical pain
Jesus suffered during the Passion. And as the mob
took their prisoner from the Garden, the disciples
fled. All of them.

"And they all forsook him, and fled," wrote Mark
(14:50).

This writer then adds a curious bit of information not found in the other Gospels. "There happened to be a young man among Jesus' followers
who wore nothing but a linen shirt. They seized
him, but he left the shirt in their hands and took to
his heels stark naked" (14:51-52, Phillips).

What is the genesis of this story? I think Judas
first led the gang to the Upper Room, thinking to
take Jesus there. Finding that he had gone, the
traitor took his "friends" to the Garden of Gethsemane where he knew Jesus was accustomed to
pray. The Upper Room, many traditions say, belonged to Mark's family. When young John Mark

saw the mob with their clubs and swords, he quickly pulled on a shirt and followed the swinging lanterns to Gethsemane.

But now let us bring the cameras up a little
closer to this drama. The Apostle John tells us how
Jesus prayed for his disciples just before he went to
Gethsemane. Listen! "I pray for them: I pray not
for the world, but for them which thou hast given
me; for they are thine. And all mine are thine, and
thine are mine; and I am glorified in them. And
now I am no more in the world, but these are in the
world, and I come to thee. Holy Father, keep
through thine own name those whom thou hast
given me, that they may be one as we are" (John
17:9-11).

That Jesus loved his disciples with an intense,
burning, sacrificial love, no one can deny. He was
their trusted friend! And during his Passion, this
devotion towers like Mount Everest.

Jesus knew the Twelve—thoroughly. He knew
their weaknesses. He knew their strengths. He
knew their secret sins. He knew their unworthy am-
bitions. But knowing all of this, he still, as John
said, "loved them unto the end" (13:1).

The least lovable of the Twelve, of course, was
Judas Iscariot. Let us notice how Jesus loved him
and protected him right up to the end.

From the moment this radical from Kerioth
joined the little band of followers, Jesus knew that
he would betray him. Indeed, he knew it before he
came for Jesus knows all things. But never do we
read of the Master saying to a follower, "You'd better watch this Judas. Not only is he a thief, but he
will betray me. You'll see."

In the Upper Room after Satan had persuaded
Judas to betray Jesus, the Master kept prodding
Judas to go out and do it. But he did it in such a
tactful way no one knew he was referring to Judas.
It would be hard to find more gentle words than
those of Jesus on this occasion. Listen!

While washing Simon Peter's feet, Jesus said, "He that is washed needeth not save to wash his feet, but is clean every whit: and ye are clean, but not all."[2]

The "not all" referred to Judas, but no one other than the traitor knew what Jesus meant.

The Master's next prod was a little stronger. He said, "He that eateth bread with me hath lifted up his heel against me" (John 13:18).

The next one was a trifle stronger: "Verily, verily, I say unto you, that one of you shall betray me" (v. 21).

Up until this time no one but Jesus and Judas knew who the traitor was. Curiously, Peter motioned for John to listen, and enquired of him whom the man might be. John was the ideal person to ask, for he was sitting next to Jesus.

The question was now on the floor, and if Jesus had been like most of us, he would have pointed to Judas and snapped, "There he is. . . . I trusted him. I taught him. I sent him out to preach. I have eaten with him and provided his food. Yes, there he is—the miserable ungrateful wretch!"

But Jesus did not do that. Instead, he said, "He it is, to whom I shall give a sop, when I have dipped it" (v. 26). Jesus then dipped the thin piece of bread squeezed into the form of a spoon and handed it to Judas. Customarily, dipping a morsel of food into a dish and then handing it to someone was considered a sign of deep friendship.

Judas took the sop. Then with a friendly, parting glance, Jesus said, "That thou doest, do quickly" (v. 27).

During all this time none of the other disciples guessed that Judas was the man. John tells us, "Now no man at the table knew for what intent he spake this unto him. For some of them thought, because Judas had the bag, that Jesus had said unto

[2] See John 13:10-29 for this episode.

him, Buy those things that we have need of against
the feast; or, that he should give something to the
poor" (vs. 28-29).

No, the Lord Jesus Christ would not lend a hand
in wrecking the man's reputation with a glance, a
word, a silence, or a nod. Jesus came to save. Not to
destroy!

Imagine how thoroughly vile, how utterly con-
temptible, and how absolutely rotten Judas must
have been when in the Garden of Gethsemane he
approached Jesus with a smile, an embrace, a kiss,
and a "Hail, Master"!

Surely a man, held in the coils of a python and
staring into its cold, greedy eyes with the knowledge that it was going to crush and devour him
would have a far more pleasant sight than did
Jesus when he looked into the dark, scheming and
hypocritical eyes of Judas Iscariot.

But what was Jesus' reaction to this vile creature
that walked and dressed like a man? Jesus accepted his smile, embrace, salutation, and kiss. Then he
returned the greeting by saying affectionately,
"Friend."

Oh, what a Christ! Oh, what a Savior! Oh, what a
Lord!

But now let us return briefly to the three disciples in the Garden. While Jesus prayed, they slept.
While Jesus agonized, they slept. While Jesus
poured out his heart, they slept. While Jesus sweat
as it were drops of blood, they slept.

He awakened them three times. They knew very
well that we was going through indescribable
agony. Even so, they slept!

Finally, however, when the mob came and arrested Jesus, they managed to stay awake and take
their places by his side—in the shadows. Their actions were utterly reprehensible. Jesus had every
human right to be thoroughly disgusted. A person
who cannot stay awake and pray with you when
you are going through the deepest trial of your life

is not much of a person. But what did Jesus do? Did he scold them? Did he forsake them? He did not!

Instead, he said to the arresting officers, ". . . if therefore ye seek me, let these go their way" (John 18:8).

While Jesus was thus speaking, Peter swung his sword at the head of Malchus. Instantly, automatically, for they were trained soldiers, the Romans reached for their swords. If Jesus had left his disciples alone, there would have been a massacre. The disciples only had two swords; the Romans had many. In the fight that would have followed, many of the once sleepy disciples would have perished, and Jesus could have escaped—as he had escaped on two occasions before.

But Jesus stopped the bloodbath by saying to Peter, "Put up thy sword into the sheath: the cup which my Father hath given me, shall I not drink it?" (v. 11).

Oh, what a Christ! Oh, what a Savior! Oh, what a Lord! Yes, he "loved them unto the end."

We do not know much about Malchus except that he was the servant of the high priest, Joseph Caiaphas. But we know that as this drama was going on in the Garden, Caiaphas was arranging for false witnesses to testify against Jesus. Malchus was engaged in a sordid business. His hands oozed with the grime of the hour. Perhaps he had been instrumental in gathering the mob, and this may be the reason he was attacked by Peter. Perhaps he had even counted out the betrayal price into the cupped hands of Judas. We do not know. But we do know that Jesus did not owe him an obligation. But what did the Master do? The Master touched his ear, and made it new.

Oh, what a Christ! Oh, what a Savior! Oh, what a Lord!

Jesus loved to preach great doctrines. But he stubbornly insisted that those who preach a doctrine should practice it. He respected the proverb, "Physician, heal thyself."

One wonders why Jesus did not allow his followers to stay asleep in the Garden. The answer is simple. Had he allowed them to sleep, they would not have seen him practice his doctrines under the most terrific pressure any man has ever been called to bear. Jesus' actions on that terrible-wonderful day were among the most effective sermons he ever preached. Years later when the apostles faced death, they remembered how Jesus faced his death. And they faced theirs with courage.

When the Lord called the first Adam in the Garden of Eden, the man hid. But when he called the second Adam in the Garden of Gethsemane, he said, "Not my will but thine." Jesus submitted to the mob so that we could be freed from the mob and so that there could be salvation for the mob.

Oh, what a Christ! Oh, what a Savior! Oh, what a Lord!

CHAPTER III

BEFORE CAIAPHAS

And they that had laid hold on Jesus led him away to Caiaphas the high priest, where the scribes and the elders were assembled. But Peter followed him afar off unto the high priest's palace, and went in, and sat down with the servants, to see the end.
—Matthew 26:57-58.

The moment Jesus was bound by the mob in Gethsemane and led away, the disciples fled—all twelve of them. Judas fled because of what he had done. The other eleven fled because of what the mob had done.

But Peter and John had not gone far before they realized that they were doing a very cowardly thing. They had failed Jesus miserably by going to sleep three times while he groaned in travail, and Peter knew in his heart that he had failed him by swinging his sword. Both he and John decided then and there that they would never fail him again.

With heavy regret, they changed their course and began to follow the Nazarene—at a safe distance!

In order to get a complete picture of the Passion, one has to read all four Gospel writers and piece their writings together. Each writer mentions a significant fact not mentioned by the other three. Matthew is the only one who mentioned the suicide

of Judas in the Gospels.[1] Mark is the only one who
mentioned the young man who fled naked. Luke is
the only one who related that Jesus looked at Peter
from the balcony of the palace of Caiaphas. And
John is the only one who mentioned that Jesus was
taken before Annas.

But all of them, yes all of them—Matthew,
Mark, Luke, and John—made a point to mention
that Peter followed Jesus. Mark, Luke, and John
did not consider the traitor's suicide important
enough to mention. But the memory of the always
impulsive, always rash, quick-to-speak, quick-to-re-
buke, quick-to-repent Simon Peter following Jesus
at such a time—even at a safe distance—was much
too thrilling to neglect. That was a scene that had to
be written!

His hands secured behind his back and pulled
painfully high between his shoulders, Jesus was led
by the officers out of the Garden of Gethsemane,
across the stone bridge that arched the Kidron, and
into the city. It is likely that the group entered the
city by means of the same gate through which
Jesus had passed with the Eleven a few hours before.

The party continued on the now near-silent
streets until they came to the imposing palace of
Annas, an extremely wealthy Sadducee. Although
seventy-year-old Annas was no longer high priest,
he was a man of great consequence. He had become
rich through Temple corruption, and his steely fingers were in many a stew—both political and other-
wise.

In spite of the fact that the high priest was appointed by Rome, Annas had managed to have five
of his sons appointed to this lucrative office. And
the present high priest, Joseph Caiaphas, was his
son-in-law.

Enemies of Annas whispered that the Romans

---

[1] Luke mentions it in Acts 1: 16-20.

gave him what he wanted because of the vast sums
of money which he had lent them.

Tottering old Annas examined Jesus briefly and
then sent him on to Caiaphas. What Annas may
have said to or asked of Jesus we do not know. It is
surmised that he was taken to Annas in order to
give Caiaphas time to gather a quorum of the Sanhedrin into his palace.

Caiaphas wanted everything to be legal, and to
get the necessary twenty-three men that early in
the morning, just before the Passover, might not be
easy.

The palace of the high priest was close to the
Upper Room. It was a magnificent building with an
outer and inner court. There was a large porch and
balcony which was supported by heavy, marble
arches.

The mob led Jesus through the gate and up onto
the balcony where he faced Caiaphas—the one who
had arranged the betrayal.

As the crowd entered the gate, John slipped in
with them; but by some curious misfortune Simon
Peter was left on the outside. This would never do,
and John knew it.

John, who was well known to the high priest and
his servants,[2] went to the girl at the gate and asked
her to let Peter in. And this she did. There was a
charcoal fire burning toward the center of the yard,
and the officers and servants were warming their
hands by the glow of the coals.

Peter knew that his safety with this mob which
was determined to murder Jesus with a frill of le-
gality thrown in, was in mingling with them—to be
lost in the crowd. And so he boldly stepped forward
and held his big fisherman's hands over the fire.

From this squatting position he could see Jesus

---

[2] It is thought that John had had a branch office in Jerusalem through which he had supplied fish to the High
Priest.

on the balcony standing before Caiaphas, and at
the same time—if necessary—he could melt into the
shadows. It was an ideal arrangement.

Suddenly someone tossed some dried thorns onto
the brazier and a bright, crimson flame shot up,
lighting the area around the coals with almost the
brilliance of day.

Then tragedy struck.

Before the flame had settled, the girl who had
opened the gate was peering into Peter's face. In
cool, even tones she said, "Art not thou also one of
this man's disciples?" (John 18:17).

"No, I am not!" he exploded, his dark eyes flashing points of flame.

Then, before anyone else could embarrass him
with another question, he strode over to the porch
and began to pace back and forth. His nerves were
raw. He was ashamed of the way he had lied, gone
to sleep, cut off the man's ear, and fled.

One can sense Peter's nervousness by the way
the Gospel writers report the event. Matthew says,
". . . and [he] went in, and sat with the servants"
(26:58).

Mark remembers, ". . . Peter was beneath in the
palace . . ." (14:66).

And John reports, "Simon Peter stood and
warmed himself" (18:25).

No, these are not contradictions! Each writer
was correct! The truth is that Cephas, the Rock,
just wasn't himself! He sat for a while. Then he
stood up. Next he crouched low. And then he paced
back and forth like a caged animal.

Presently, while he was striding back and forth
on the marble porch, he heard footsteps. He whirled
to see what it was. The steps were those of the men
who were gathering to try Jesus.

Peter felt a lump in his throat and his hands became damp with sweat as the men gathered. In that
crowd of determined, curious men were leading
priests, elders, and members of the Sanhedrin.

If Peter had hoped there would not be a quorum, he was in for a letdown. As inconvenient as it was to get up at that dreadful hour in the morning, the officials assembled. Mark reports, ". . . and with him were assembled all the chief priests and the elders and the scribes" (14:53).

How hard it is to get a crowd to worship God! But how easy it is to get a crowd to condemn a man!

About this time, while Peter was out on the porch, another girl cornered him and, speaking loudly so that the men about her could hear, she said, pointing to Peter, "This fellow was also with Jesus of Nazareth" (Matt. 26:71).

Peter's face, in spite of the cold, turned crimson. Then, with uncontrolled anger, he fairly shouted, "I do not know the man" (v. 72).

And, in addition to the lie, he seared his lips with an oath.

While this was going on, Jesus was being examined privately by Caiaphas.

Peter now returned to the fire, for not only was there a chill in the air, but there was also a chill in his heart.

He had denied the Lord twice!

During those terrible pre-dawn hours Jesus taught some profound lessons, and so let us climb the steps to the balcony and see what was taking place.

One time Jesus had said to his disciples, "But beware of men: for they will deliver you up to the councils, and they will scourge you in their synagogues; and ye shall be brought before governors and kings for my sake, for a testimony against them and the Gentiles. But when they deliver you up, take no thought how or what ye shall speak: for it shall be given you in that same hour what ye shall speak" (Matt. 10:17-19). And now Jesus was demonstrating just how to do this.

Jesus had trusted completely in the Father, and since he had surrendered to him in the Garden a few hours before, he was utterly calm. Indeed, Jesus was about the only calm person in the entire palace of the high priest! Let us, however, view the scene.

Still bound by ropes, Jesus stood in front of Caiaphas. His long, white robe may have been soiled from his agonizing prayers in Gethsemane. His feet also were probably dirty, for there had been no way to wash them. Moreoever, he had walked from the Upper Room to Gethsemane and then back again.

In contrast, Joseph Caiaphas was immaculately dressed in his scarlet, purple, and gold robes of office. He wore a turban-shaped linen miter on his head. Precious stones gleamed on his shoulders, and twelve flashing jewels winked and sparkled on his chest.

Leaning forward, the high priest asked Jesus clever questions about his disciples and his doctrines. Perhaps the cunning man not only planned to be rid of Jesus, but his disciples as well. Like his father-in-law, he was a schemer.

Caiaphas found it impossible to forgive Jesus for driving the money-changers from the Temple. A portion of the exchange commissions stuck to his fingers; and like moderns, he resented anyone who touched his pocketbook!

Jesus never involved the Twelve in his trial. He loved them passionately, and did not want them harmed. He replied politely to his interrogator and to one question he answered, "I spake openly in the world; I ever taught in the synagogue, and in the temple, whither the Jews always resort; and in secret have I said nothing. Why askest thou me? ask them which heard me, what I have said unto them: behold, they know what I said.'"

All at once, and without any reason, a nearby of-

' See John 18:20-23 for this episode.

ficer smashed Jesus in the mouth with his opened
palm and angrily demanded, "Answerest thou the
high priest so?"

To this insult, Jesus replied calmly, "If I have
spoken evil, bear witness of the evil: but if well,
why smitest thou me?"

The treatment was cruel and unjust. But it did
not shake Jesus. He had prepared for it in Gethsemane!

Not only was Jesus calm. He was also very pa-
tient. Soon the chambers were filled with those who
had come to try him. These men took their seats,
yawned; and the public trial began. Witnesses were
called to testify against the prisoner, but they so
contradicted themselves that Matthew labeled
them "false witnesses."

Perjury, on that terrible night, was a very common commodity and was produced with little
thought—and less effort.

Finally, two false witnesses came forward with a
story based on a misunderstanding. With all the
pomp they could muster they pointed accusing fingers at Jesus and sneered, "This fellow said, I am
able to destroy the temple of God, and to build it in
three days" (Matt. 26:61).

Yes, Jesus had said that. But the temple he had
referred to was his own body, not the Temple that
was being built by Herod to please the Jews. But
even if he had referred to Herod's temple, the remark would certainly not have been a crime worthy
of death! This odd charge, however, was undoubtedly just a fragment of the ridiculous and unjust
accusations that were hurled at him.

This trial could not have been accepted by any
superior court worthy of the name. According to
the law Jesus should have been arrested by those
who witnessed against him. This was not done.

According to the law the Sanhedrin was supposed to meet in a regular designated place. This
was not done.

According to the law the charges against Jesus should have been read at the beginning of the trial. This was not done.

According to the law the prisoner could not be examined before the trial. This was done.

The foundation stones of this trial were lies. They were laid in the slime of perjury by the criminal hands of false witnesses, and they formed a quaking structure that was illegally built.

But how did Jesus react to all of this? He was calm. He had prepared in the Garden of Gethsemane. Oh, the marvelous understanding and patience of the Lord Jesus Christ!

During this ordeal Jesus' face had become swollen from the blow he had received from the officer. But his countenance was not lined with resentment, or marked with care, or pale with fear. Jesus preached that his Father cared for the sparrows, and that he tallied the number of hairs on the heads of the people. He was now demonstrating to the world that this was true.

Those who seek healing of the body look to the wounds of Christ.

Those who seek salvation look to the blood of Christ.

Those who seek the infilling of the Holy Spirit look to the commands of Christ.

Those who seek calmness, patience, understanding, humility, and trust should study the trial of Christ.

Your trial may be very great. But does it compare to the trial of Jesus? Look to him. He will supply all the grace[4] you need. The supply of grace is exhaustless, without end. Take hold of that grace by faith[5] and you will be utterly amazed at the strength that will flow into your life.

[4] **G** od's
   R edemption
   A t
   C hrist's
   E xpense

[5] **F** orever
   A ll
   I s
   T hrough
   H im

Indeed, it will invigorate your entire being!

As Jesus looked into the face of Caiaphas, he knew that God was having his way. Days before this, the high priest had inadvertently made a statement that was full of profound good-news truth. Said he to the assembled Sanhedrin, "It is expedient for us, that one man should die for the people, and that the whole nation perish not" (John 11:50).

Caiaphas glared at Jesus. He searched his mind for an item with which he could convict him. Then he got an idea. Making a gesture toward him, he said, "I adjure thee by the living God, that thou tell us whether thou be the Christ, the Son of God" (Matt. 26:63).

This was the Jewish form of oath, and every Jew was required to answer. Jesus was a law-abiding man and so he replied promptly.

"I am," he said without hesitation.

His answer was definite. He claimed to be the Son of God. And he was!

Jesus had barely uttered these words when the high priest leaped to his feet and ripped his robes from the neck downward. He ripped them so thoroughly they could not be repaired. He did this because it was the traditional thing to do when blasphemy was uttered. Jesus had affirmed that he was the Son of God, and Caiaphas considered this blasphemy!

Again Caiaphas did not know it; but his actions had preached a New Testament, landmark truth. And that truth was that the days of the old high priest were over. The writer of the Book of Hebrews enlarges that thought like this, "Seeing then that we have a great high priest, that is passed into the heavens, Jesus the Son of God, let us hold fast our profession. For we have not an high priest which cannot be touched with the feelings of our infirmities; but was in all points tempted like as we are, yet without sin" (Heb. 4:14-15).

As the robes of Caiaphas lay about him in shreds he faced the Sanhedrin and fairly hissed, "He hath spoken blasphemy; what further need have we of witnesses? behold, now ye have heard his blasphemy. What think ye?"[6]

The puppet assembly replied at once, and in unison, like an ancient Greek chorus, "He is guilty of death."

This proclamation unleashed the very worst characteristics in the crowd. Instantly they began to make sport of Jesus. They slapped him. They spat on him. They knocked him about. They blindfolded him, punched him, and then demanded that he tell them who struck the blow.

While this was going on, Simon Peter was at the fire warming himself. But he could hear the sinister jeers, the coarse laughter, and even the sound of the blows. The big fisherman had been unusually nervous all morning. But now after he heard the cry, "He is guilty of death," his nervousness increased. He responded by huddling closer to the flames and chattering about many things of little importance.

Then suddenly a girl who was near him exclaimed, "Surely thou art also one of them; for thy speech betrayeth thee" (v. 74).

Poor Peter! He just could not keep his mouth shut. Nor could he keep from slurring his gutterals and swallowing his syllables. His Galilean accent was as plain as the mast of his boat.

He turned to the girl angrily. His face was livid, distorted, embarrassed. His lips curled and his broad shoulders shook with passion. He began to swear with vile, bloodcurdling fishermen's oaths. His black eyes became volcanoes of anger while he shouted hoarsely, "I know not the man."

He had just spat out the last denial when somewhere in the distance a cock stretched itself, lifted

---

[6] See Matthew 26:65-74 for this episode.

its wings, and crowed. Nervously Peter turned his head to discover the source of the sound, and as he did so he saw the dawn creeping "in silver sandled feet" over the Mount of Olives.

Then he remembered!

Yes, Jesus had said, "Before the cock crow twice, thou shalt deny me thrice" (Mark 14:30). Immediately hot, bitter tears filled his eyes and plummeted down his weather-beaten cheeks.

At this precise moment, Peter turned toward the balcony. Jesus was standing there. His hands were still bound. His face was swollen and blotched with purple bruises. Dried spittle was on his cheeks. His hair and beard were matted. Now, as Peter looked, he knew that Jesus had heard every word he had said—including those terrible oaths.

Peter wished he were dead!

And then a wonderful thing happened. Jesus began to look at Peter; and the eyes of the Master and those of the fisherman met, and held—for a long time. These eyes of Jesus were soft with kindness, forgiveness, understanding, love, and unutterable compassion.

But soon Jesus was jerked away by a guard. Peter, however, never forgot that look. It stirred a recent memory. Yes, it came storming back to him now. Jesus had said, "I have prayed for thee, that thy faith fail not" (Luke 22:32).

On that glorious and terrible morning the old Simon died and the new Peter began to live!

CHAPTER IV.

PILATE'S BASIN

*When Pilate saw that he could prevail nothing,
but that rather a tumult was made, he took water,
and washed his hands before the multitude, saying,
I am innocent of the blood of this just person: see
ye to it*—Matthew 27:24.

The most despised name since the Crucifixion is
Judas Iscariot. Before the death of Jesus, it was a
very popular name, for it had been the name of the
Jewish George Washington—Judas Maccabeus
who had won the nation's independence from the
Syrians and restored the worship of Jehovah in
Jerusalem.

Two of Jesus' disciples and a blood brother were
named Judas. But because of the traitor the name
is seldom used in our time.

The next most despised name is Pontius Pilate,
the name of the ex-cavalry officer who delivered
Jesus to the mob to be crucified. Few mothers
would want to name a son after him!

But, alas, the characteristics associated with
these two names have not disappeared. The number
of people in our world with traits comparable to
Judas Iscariot is, thank God, small. But although
we hate to admit it, there are hundreds of millions
on this orbiting planet of ours with the main
character-weakness of the Roman procurator, Pontius Pilate. And that weakness is the reluctance to

45

stand for that which is right in the teeth of the crowd. And many of these people have mailing addresses in your town and mine! About the only difference between them and Pilate is that he mumbled his excuses in Latin and they mumble theirs in English.

But, let us take a look at this spineless man in action. The scene took place on the fifteenth day of Nisan in the Jewish year, 3790. This would be Friday[1], April 7, A.D. 29 in our way of reckoning. It was, perhaps, 8:00 A.M. The sun was shining over the Mount of Olives, bathing the tall columns of the Temple in its warm light.

Pilate, on that fateful morning in the Roman year A.U.C. 783, was sitting in a regal chair placed on a stone landing near the Praetorium—the judgment hall near the Tower of Antonia.

A man of fashion, his hair was closely cropped in the Roman way, and defiant guards stood on either side with heavy spears in their right hands. Pilate had reason to be happy. As the fifth procurator of Judea, Samaria, and Idumea, he was a privileged character. Governors of distant provinces in the Roman Empire were not allowed to take their wives along. But an exception had been made with him. Claudia Procula had been by his side ever since he had been elevated to that office in A.D. 26. Perhaps Claudia had insisted. As the granddaughter of the great Augustus and the illegitimate daughter of Tiberius Caesar's third wife, she had influence in Rome.

With care and good luck, Pilate might be promoted!

---

[1] The dates of the Passover and crucifixion have been the source of endless debate. Many contend that Jesus could not have been crucified on Friday since he was resurrected on Sunday morning, and thus could not have been in the tomb for three days and three nights. In my opinion, however, I believe that the strongest arguments support the traditional date of Friday.

But this morning the Procurator's dark Roman eyes glistened with sullen anger. He was annoyed at the huge crowd of Jews who milled around on the Roman parade ground out in front. Fearing defilement, they refused to come up close and speak to him man-to-man. They acted as if he was beneath them, or had bad breath.

Not only did Pilate have to put up with the constant stench of sacrificial animals—during Nero's reign in A.D. 65, 256,500 lambs were slaughtered in the Passover season—but in addition he had to be extremely careful not to interfere with their religion. And during this Passover season they were extremely touchy.

To the Jews the Passover season was the highlight of the year; and across the centuries the period had grown in popularity. The Feast of Unleavened Bread had become attached to it, and by this time the combined feasts lasted a total of eight days. With this popularity, many legends surrounded the festival. For example, it was believed that the walls of Jericho fell on this date; and that it was during this period that the mysterious writing appeared on the wall in Babylon.

Fear of defilement was heavy in the hearts of the Jews that morning. They did not fear being unable to partake of the Paschal lamb; for they had already done that the night before on the 14th of Nisan—the night of Jesus' Last Supper with the disciples in the Upper Room. But there were other ceremonies ahead, notably the second day of the presentation of the Chagigah on that very day, the 15th of Nisan.

Since Jerusalem was the only place in Israel where these ceremonies could be celebrated, enormous throngs packed the city. And in preparation for this, workers had been employed a month before to get the roads in repair and to make certain that all the sepulchers had been whitened. The marking of the sepulchers was considered extremely impor-

tant, for if anyone touched something that per-
tained to death, that person was considered un-
clean and was excluded from the celebrations.

And now the "ceremoniously-clean" leaders of
the mob sent a Gentile messenger to Pilate to in-
form him that they had some extremely important
business to transact with him. Soon the proceedings
started. Then the stocky procurator enquired,
"What accusation bring ye against this man?"
(John 18:29).

Pilate's question was immediately answered by a
well-oiled statement that had obviously been re-
hearsed. "If he were not a malefactor, we would not
have delivered him up to thee" (v. 30). And as they
said this, Jesus was shoved forward so that Pilate
could see him more clearly.

Toward the front of this huge parade ground, referred to as Gabbatha by John, the lines of a game
had been scratched into one of the large pavement
stones. Bored soldiers, tired of drilling, liked to
gamble here. In a favorite game, the winner was
dubbed "king for a day." And it is quite possible
that as Jesus was being tried, some soldiers were
busy tossing dice by his side. After all, a trial before
Pilate was a common thing.

As Pilate peered down at Jesus, I think he knew
in his heart that Jesus was innocent. And, moreover, I think he admired him. He had heard what
Jesus had had to say about the coin with the image
on it, and, hearing it, had smiled. Jesus of Nazareth
was a man after his own heart!

But then he shifted his eyes from the innocent
Jesus bound with ropes to the pompous Caiaphas
surrounded with power. Pilate knew that if he did
the right thing he would free Jesus. But he also
knew that if he freed the Nazarene, he would have
to deal with Annas, Caiaphas, the elders, the rich
Sadducees, and a host of others who had power. At
the time, Emperor Tiberius was living a life of de-
bauchery on the Island of Capri, and Pilate did not

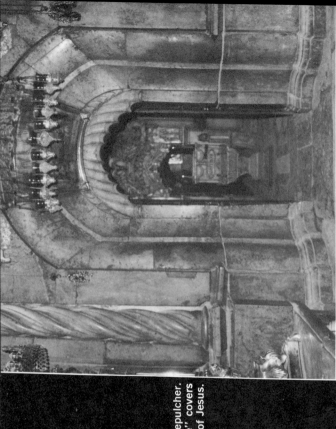

The Church of the Holy Sepulcher.
The "Large Dome" covers
the "tomb" of Jesus.

The Upper Room.

An olive press—symbolic of Jesus' suffering.

Within the Garden of Gethsemane.

The Dome of the Rock—site of Herod's Temple.

Game scratched on the pavement—where Jesus faced Pilate.

The Ecce Homo Arch.
Here Pilate said of Jesus,
"Behold the Man."

The Damascus gate—Jesus passed through here on the way to his Crucifixion.

Modern crosses can be lovely—but none can indicate the suffering Jesus endured at Calvary.

(Photo—Israel Government Tourist Office)

The Wailing Wall.

A fiisherman at the Sea of Galilee.
(Photo—Israel Government Tourist Office)

A street in Old Jerusalem.

The Empty Tomb.

want to offend him with even the hint of trouble. He knew that Tiberius was in the habit of ordering executions with the same carelessness one would have in swatting a fly. As he pondered these things, Pilate decided to play it safe. He would be neutral.

"Take ye him, and judge him according to your law," he said. But the Jews would have none of this. "It is not lawful for us to put any man to death," they said (v. 31).

Pilate should have learned there and then that no one—I mean no one—can be neutral about Jesus. But he did not. He felt certain that someplace there was a neutral corner where he could continue to play with his toys unmolested!

Slipping down from his seat to the pavement, Pilate motioned Jesus into the judgment hall. There he could speak to him privately. He had heard strange stories about the carpenter—stories of blind eyes opening, of mute voices singing, of the insane becoming sane, of lepers being cleansed, of the multitudes being fed. He wanted to have a face-to-face conversation with Jesus—a conversation that would not be overheard by the itching ears of Caiaphas.

And there in the ornate judgment hall the former officer in a Roman legion met Jesus Christ face-to-face. Pilate, perhaps a little playfully, asked, "Art thou the King of the Jews?" (v. 33).

Jesus answered, "My kingdom is not of this world: if my kingdom were of this world, then would my servants fight, that I should not be delivered to the Jews" (v. 36).

Pilate was not quite satisfied with that answer and so he pressed the point a little further. "Art thou a king then?"

To this, Jesus' reply was prompt and to the point. "To this end was I born, and for this cause came I into the world, that I should bear witness unto the truth. Every one that is of the truth heareth my voice" (v. 37).

"What is truth?" asked the procurator a little startled.

But then without waiting for an answer, for he probably felt none was possible, Pilate strode out of the hall. "I find no fault in him," he said.

The reply was a storm of protest. Shaking their fists in the air, the mob piled one accusation on top of another.

Had Pilate really believed in Jesus, he would have said, "I find no fault in him. I am releasing him, and anyone who bothers him will be prosecutted." But Pilate did not have the couarge to say that. Caiaphas was too near!

As Jesus stood behind or by the side of the Roman procurator and the people hurled their wanton lies at him, he was completely silent. Indeed, his silence was so obvious Pilate commented, "Hearest thou not how many things they witness against thee?" And when Jesus persisted in his silence, we are told that "the governor marvelled greatly" (Matt. 27:14).

Although Jesus' lips and vocal cords were silent, he actually was preaching a sermon—a sermon in silence. That sermon was a dramatic answer to Pilate's question, "What is truth?" In plain English it said, "Pontius Pilate, I am the truth. You cannot be neutral about me; nor can anyone else!"

As the people were denouncing Jesus, Pilate suddenly heard the word *Galilee*. The word brought a quick smile to his lips, for this was a sure way to a neutral corner! Jesus, he discovered, was a Galilean. Pilate had no jurisdiction over Galilee. That authority belonged to Herod; and Herod, by fortunate circumstances, happened to be in Jerusalem at that very moment.

Pilate's problem of being neutral was solved, and the solution was as simple as two plus two. Licking his lips in satisfaction, he gave orders for Jesus to be taken to Herod.

As the mob led the Nazarene away, Pilate must

have rubbed his hands together in glee. He had escaped making a decision. It was wonderful. He was delighted.

But now let us see what happened when Jesus faced the ruler of Galilee.

It was quite natural for Herod to want to see Jesus, for it was his father, Herod the Great, who had murdered the little children in Bethlehem in his attempt to kill the infant Jesus. And he is the one who was denounced by John the Baptist, a cousin of Jesus, for incestuously marrying his niece Herodias, a former wife of his half-brother.

Being a Galilean, Jesus knew him well and characterized him as "that fox."

When Jesus was placed in front of King Herod, this ruler of Galilee was most anxious to see him. He hoped to get Jesus to entertain him by making a sign or performing a miracle. The Jews were having a good time at Passover, and so why shouldn't he?

But Jesus refused to perform a miracle or even answer a question. He clothed himself in a dignified silence. But the silence was shattered by the chief priests and scribes who spewed out a mighty stream of accusations.

At this point, remembering history, it is easy to see how Jesus could have instantly freed himself with a quick statement or two. In order to understand this, we must go back to Herod the Great. Having executed a brigand without first obtaining permission from the Sanhedrin, that powerful body had denounced him. Later, when his power was more secure, Herod recalled forty-five members of the Sanhedrin and had them slaughtered. Then he confiscated their estates and replaced them with another forty-five men of his own choosing so that the body again would have its required seventy-one members.

With this as a background, Jesus might have remarked, "Your father also had trouble with the

Sanhedrin." And that remark alone might have convinced King Herod of the injustice that was being attempted by the Jews.

But Jesus doggedly refused to defend himself.

Enraged by his silence, Herod and his soldiers mocked Jesus and clothed him in a purple robe. Then they returned him to Pilate.

The procurator was keenly disappointed when Jesus was returned, for he had considered the trial to be over. Many in the mob also must have assumed this, for when Jesus was brought back to the pavement, Pilate "called together the chief priests and the rulers and the people."[2]

When they were all assembled, Pilate held up his hand for silence, and then he said to them, "Ye have brought this man unto me, as one that perverteth the people: and, behold, I, having examined him before you, have found no fault in this man touching those things whereof ye accuse him" (v. 14).

He then paused while he swept his eyes over the crowd. Then he added, "No, nor yet Herod: for I sent you to him; and, lo, nothing worthy of death is done unto him" (v. 15).

The faces of the multitude below him, however, did not respond gracefully. Instead, a storm began to brew. They began to bubble and froth. Only a death sentence could satisfy them!

Again Pilate learned that he could not be neutral, and the voice of silence repeated its sermon, "Pontius Pilate, I am the truth. You cannot be neutral about me. Nor can anyone else!"

Pilate frowned as he tried to find another way of escape in making a decision about Christ. And then a clever new scheme formed in his mind. It was customary during the period of the Passover to release a prisoner as part of the ritual. "Perhaps," he rea-

[2] See Luke 23:13-15 for this episode.

soned, "I will be able to get the crowd to ask for Jesus."

And in order to assure himself that the crowd would choose Jesus, he chose the most despicable prisoner he could find and stood him side by side with the Nazarene.

Barabbas was a murderer and a robber. He has been pictured as having snarling lips, protruding and missing teeth, bloodshot eyes, and an animal-like face. Some of the early manuscripts indicate that his first name was Jesus. Thus the choice before the crowd was a dramatic one. It was either Jesus Barabbas or Jesus Christ!

But before Pilate could put the proposition to them, a servant rushed up and put a note in his hand. A quick reading caused his heart to pound. The fine writing from his wife said, "Have thou nothing to do with that just man: for I have suffered many things this day in a dream because of him" (Matt. 27:19).

Pilate crumpled the parchment angrily in his powerful fingers. But even this pressure did not keep his hand from trembling. There was indeed something most unusual about this prisoner! But with an effort like that of freeing a lion from a trap he pushed his wife's warning out of his mind.

"Wither of the twain will ye that I release unto you?" (v. 21), he demanded, as he vainly tried to keep a quiver out of his voice.

The mob's answer bounced back immediately. "Away with this man, and release unto us Barabbas" (Luke 23:18). Careless with their emotions, the crowd acted like famished animals snapping for food.

Pilate found again that he could not be neutral. He just had to make a decision. And again the voice of silence repeated its sermon, "Pontius Pilate, I am the truth. You cannot be neutral about me. Nor can anyone else!"

But the ex-cavalry officer would not give up.

There must a way of neutrality, or at least near-neutrality! If only he could think of something. And then a compromise slithered into his mind. Maybe this new idea would help him—at least in the eyes of Claudia.

The idea was to have Jesus scourged.

Maybe this would satisfy the majority of the crowd and allow him eventually to free the Nazarene. At least the scourging would not weigh as heavily on his soul as crucifixion. With this thought in mind, he gave the order.

Jewish scourging was dubbed "intermediate death" and was inflicted with a long, supple rod. The victim was given thirteen stripes on the left shoulder; thirteen on the right; and thirteen across the thighs.

Roman scourging was much more severe and was known as "halfway death." It was administered by an expert. This trained man used a whip called a flagellum. It had a stubby wooden handle to which was attached a bundle of leather thongs. A bit of bone or chain was tied to the end of each thong.

Pilate was a Roman. Jesus had been "tried" in a Roman court. The sentence therefore was halfway death—a punishment illegal for uncondemned Roman citizens.

Jesus was taken to the whipping post. The charge was read. Then his hands were tied around the post and his back was bared.

Syrian soldiers standing nearby sneered, "So this is the king of the Jews! Some king! Look at his swollen eyes! Look at his puffed, distorted cheeks! Look at the saliva on his face! Look at his tangled hair, his matted beard. One can see anything in Jerusalem. Just anything!"

The professional administrator of halfway death picked up the flagellum with the care of a symphonic conductor picking up a baton. Next he carefully took his stand so that the bits of bones and chain on the end of the thongs would do the maximum

damage. This was an art and he prided himself in
knowing just how to do it. After adjusting his
stance, first this way and then that, he was ready.
Then, his feet spread, he lifted the whip. There was
a strain on his face as he sucked in air for the blow.

With his biceps bunched like springing cats, he
brought down the whip. The leather thongs sang
through the air and scooped long, crimson furrows
on the back of Jesus. Up and down, up and down,
went the whip. As he warmed to his task, the blows
became stronger and the body of Jesus sank lower
and lower on the post.

The soldiers watched with amusement. Each
groan brought a shout of laughter and an encour-
agement to strike harder. "Oh, come on. You can
do better than that. Remember he's a king, and as
a king he deserves the best you have. That's right,
strike harder!"

But all the soldiers didn't get involved. Many
were just too bored, or were considering the assig-
nation they had planned. Some of them slept. One
man drew a filthy picture in the dust with his toe.
Another yawned and made the music of a filthy
song as he stifled the yawn with the palm of his
hand. Others gossiped.

Finally the professional was tired. Jesus' back
was raw, and the professional knew that if he continued his victim would lose consciousness and not
feel the pain. And this, of course, would ruin the
fun. And so he stopped.

Now the soldiers put a royal robe around Jesus.
Dry thorns from a nearby bucket were hastily made
into a crown and jammed onto his head. A reed was
thrust into his hand. Then they struck him with
their fists. They slapped him, churned more spittle
in their mouths, and spat it on his face.

One man hit him over the head with the reed,
thus driving the brittle thorns into his flesh. By
now blood was streaming down his face from the
wounds.

Then once again Jesus was stood before Pilate. This time the procurator hoped the crowd was satisfied. Lifting the hand of Jesus, he faced the crowd and cried, "Behold the man" (John 19:5).

But the people would not let him off! With their swarthy faces twisted in hate, bright with intolerance, and lined with viciousness, they shouted, "Crucify him! Crucify him! Crucify him!"

"Why, what evil hath he done?" (Mark 15:14) demanded Pilate.

Waiting only long enough to moisten their lips, the mob shouted back, "Crucify him! Crucify him! Crucify him!" And as they shouted they were so carried away with their lust for blood, they forgot the possibility of defilement. Indeed, they may have forgotten that they should not draw too close to the judgment hall and that they had to be careful of the way they spat.

On this subject tradition was very clear. If their gob of spittle landed on a dry stone it was perfectly all right. But if by chance a careless aim or a puff of wind landed it in the dust, they were in trouble. Why? Because the spittle would mix with the dust and create clay. And this was creative work. And creative work during Passover was defiling!

But Pilate was not ready to give up. Luke tells us that for the third time he begged, "Why, what evil hath he done?" (23:22).

This time the answer came like the lashing waves of a typhoon, "Crucify him! Crucify him! Crucify him!"

Pilate, however, was still determined to be neutral. He signaled, and a bowl of water and a towel were brought to him. Then, after dipping his hands in the water and drying them on the towel, he said, "I am innocent of the blood of this just person: see ye to it" Matt 27:24[3]

---

[3] Because of this statement, both Pilate and his wife are revered as saints in Ethiopia. Their feast day is June 25.

Out of the corner of his eye, Pilate watched Jesus. The man of Galilee could barely stand. His garments were crimson. The hands which had fed the thousands were now limp at his side, for by now he was so weakened no one feared his escape. The eyes which had gleamed with good humor, truth, compassion, forgiveness, and affection were like empty sockets.

Jesus did not say a word. But that silence! That terrible silence! That awful silence, preached in more articulate tones than sound could have done, "Pontius Pilate, I am the truth! You have not been neutral. You have made your decision!"

CHAPTER V.

SIMON OF CYRENE

And they compel one Simon a Cyrenian, who passed by, coming out of the country, the father of Alexander and Rufus, to bear his cross.—Mark 15:21

After Pontius Pilate had ceremonially washed his hands and declared, "I am innocent of the blood of this just person: see ye to it," the crowd was so delirious with their victory they shouted back almost gleefully, "His blood be on us, and our children" (Matt. 27:24-25). The only thing left for the mob to do now was to see that the crucifixion was carried out, and that the victim died before sundown.

Had the Jews put Jesus to death in their own way, he would have been stoned; but since they were doing it the legal way—the Roman way—he was crucified. Death by crucifixion was invented by the Persians. It was then adopted by the Carthaginians; and from them it was passed on to the Romans. And the Romans perfected it into an art—complete with a long vocabulary.

The normal cross was made of two pieces of wood, usually pine or cypress. The upright piece was the *stipes crucis*. This post-like piece was normally left permanently in the ground so that it could serve the next victim.

Two types of crosses were used. The first was the

crux humilis—the low one. These shorter crosses
were usually about six feet high. Since they were
more convenient, the executioners preferred them,
especially when there were many convicts. Another
distinct advantage of the short cross was that such
wild animals as wolves could more easily get to the
victims.

Rome's Esquiline Hill was impaled with
hundreds of these vertical posts. And this area was
frequented by more flesh-hungry animals than any
other area near the Eternal City.

The other type of cross was the *crux sublimis*.
This tall cross was used to display especially no-
torious persons such as Regulus at Carthage. Normally Romans were not crucified. But there were ex-
ceptions. When a condemned assassin in Spain
begged for mercy, pleading that he was a Roman,
Galba, recognizing his citizenship, said, "Let this
citizen hang higher than the rest, and have his cross
whitewashed." That man perished on the *crux sublimis.*

Quite often a piece of wood was nailed part way
down the *stipes*. This *sedile*, as it was called, jutted
out like a blunt horn, forming a kind of seat. The
purpose of this was, it is supposed, that the crucified could live a little longer—and thus suffer more.

History mentions a slave who was pardoned by
an emperor after he had already been nailed into
place. After his recovery, the man wrote, "On the
cross there are only two things, pain and eternity.
They tell me I was only on the cross twenty-four
hours, but I was on the cross longer than the world
existed. If there is no time, then every moment is
forever."[1]

As the mob faced Jesus, they faced a man who
was utterly worn out. After his hours of agonized
praying in Gethsemane he had gone from one weary

[1] From *Spartacus* by Howard Fast. Copyright 1951. Ban-
tam.

trial to another, and he had not had a drop of water
or a bite of food since the Last Supper, the night
before.

There had been the trial before Annas, the three
trials before Joseph Caiaphas—the preliminary
trial, the regular trial, and the repeat trial—the one
early in the morning to make everything legal and
within the letter of the law. There had been the
trial before Pilate and the trial before Herod. And
then there was the final trial before Pilate.

In addition, Jesus had gone through endless
mental and physical torture. There had been the
pain of finding Peter, James, and John asleep while
he agonized in the Garden. There had been the pain
of having Judas betray him with a kiss. There had
been the pain of having seen Peter slash off a man's
ear with a sword. There had been the pain of being
struck before Annas. There had been the pain of
the beating before Caiaphas. There had been the
pain of Peter's denial. There had been the pain of
being mocked by Herod and his soldiers. And there
had been the pain of being scourged by the order of
Pilate.

The man delivered by the procurator to the mob
was already half dead. He was a pitiful sight with
the crown of thorns on his head and his raw back
and bruised face.

Presently an order was given and two criminals
were produced and placed with Jesus. Then each
was given either the full cross or, as many scholars
think, the *patibulum*—the cross piece which would
be fastened to the stipes when they reached the
place of execution.

At a signal, a platoon of legionnaires armed with
spears formed a box around the condemned so that
none could escape. Then a man appeared with a
thin pine board. The large black letters read:
"THIS IS THE KING OF THE JEWS."[2]

[2] Luke 23:38.

The inscription was written in Latin, Hebrew, and Greek. A Roman soldier on a horse led the legionnaires, and the man with the sign took his place in front. When everything was ready the centurion on the horse barked the order, "Forward march," and the solemn procession headed for the skull-shaped hill, Calvary.

Today, the road they followed is known as the Via Dolorosa—the Way of Sorrows. At the start, the road was about twelve feet wide. The stone-paved street led up a sharp incline that sloped toward the Damascus Gate. Jesus, with the heavy wood on his houlder, did not walk as fast now as he had the day before when he led the Twelve into the Upper Room and the Eleven to the Garden of Gethsemane and the three inside the Garden. Although he had trained as a carpenter and was used to carrying many a door and beam, the weight of this cross was unusually heavy. And this heaviness was not due to the wood itself. Rather it was because the sins of the world were piled high on that burden. Indeed, the load was so heavy that no one else—giant though he might be—could even lift it.

The sins of the world are heavy!

As the newly formed column shuffled toward the grim hill of death, multitudes watched from the streets, the housetops, and the windows. Some of the dense throng jeered at the condemned. Others were silent. Some turned their heads as they dabbed at their eyes. Some yawned. Others giggled and laughed.

In that crowd, however, there must have been some whom Jesus had healed of blindness. Now, they were blind again—blind because of their tears. One can almost hear former beggars shouting frantically, "No! No! You can't do this to Jesus. He healed my eyes!"

But these cries were ignored, and the crowd plodded on.

Also in that crowd there must have been those

whom Jesus had healed of leprosy. And I think I can see them pointing with new fingers and crying out in desperation, "No! No! You can't do this to Jesus. He healed my leprosy!"

But these cries were ignored, and the crowd plodded on.

And certainly in that crowd there must have been some whom Jesus had made to hear and speak. And I think I can hear them listening to Jesus' groans and then shouting with their new voices. "You can't do this to Jesus. He healed my ears and gave me speech!"

But these cries were ignored and the crowd plodded on.

Then all at once the former carpenter of Nazareth who had had a constitution of iron began to sway under the load. Moments later he stumbled; and then he fell to the street. Someone kicked him. A Roman soldier swore. Others taunted. But he could not get up. His humanity was exhausted.

The centurion was now in a dilemma. He could not ask one of his soldiers to carry the Cross, nor could he ask a Jew to carry it. For if a Jew even touched it he would be defiled. And the centurion knew full well that the Roman law against interference in religious matters was inflexible.

One wonders where Peter, and James, and John were at this time. They would have carried the Cross. They did not need to fear partaking in at least the first part of the Passover, for they had already eaten the Last Supper with Jesus. Peter and John had been at the palace of Caiaphas a few hours before. But where were they now?

Then Simon of the city of Cyrene, a large city of North Africa, came elbowing by. His black skin gleamed in the fierce sun. Just in from the country, he was minding his own business when he was attracted by the column on its way to Calvary.

The centurion noticed him immediately. He was just the man! He snapped an order and the legion-

naires grabbed Simon and forced him to pick up
Jesus' cross.

Who was Simon of Cyrene? We cannot be certain, but we can make some good guesses. Mark
tells us that he was the father of Alexander and
Rufus (15:21). And since the Gospel according to
Mark was directed to the Romans, it may well be
that these sons were well known in the church at
Rome. Luke writes of ". . . Simeon that was called
Niger. . . ."[2] Simeon is probably the same as Simon
and, as we all know, Niger means black. It is on this
thread of thought that we guess that Simon of
Cyrene was black. Since he was from a city in Africa, and since tradition says he was black, it is reasonable to believe he was.

The greatest honor ever given to a human being
was when Mary conceived by the Holy Ghost and
gave birth to Jesus Christ. But the next greatest
honor ever given to a human being was the honor of
carrying his cross.

That honor was entirely unexpected. When
Simon left home he had no idea that he was going
to play such a vital role in history. But God's calls
are frequently unexpected.

Perhaps right now the Lord is asking you to
shoulder a seemingly impossible burden. Maybe he
is saying, "Full-time service." Or, perhaps, he is
asking you to get active in church work. Maybe
he's given you the talent to earn money and now
he's asking you to dedicate your wealth to him.
Whatever the case, do it!

Now we often hear that a cross is something that
we voluntarily pick up. But this is not always so.
The Gospels tell us that Simon was *compelled* to
carry the cross of Jesus. We must remember that
real Christians are obedient Christians; and that if
we are to obey we must willingly pick up the bur-

[2] Acts 13:1.

dens Jesus hands us—and be thankful for the privilege of carrying them!

The task Simon was asked to complete was not a very spectacular one. His job was simply to carry the Cross a few hundred feet, for strong tradition tells us that Jesus had already carried it most of the way. The job seemed quite insignificant at the time. And there was no apparent glory in complying. Moreover, there was no spectacular, advanced publicity.

It is easy enough to get people to assume crosses —crosses with publicity attached to them. But it is usually difficult to get them to assume the little crosses that are unnoticed by the crowd. And yet frequently it is the small cross that does the most good.

Sometimes we are asked to carry a cross for a very simple reason. No one else will carry it. But in this respect we are much like Simon of Cyrene. Simon was not chosen because he was pious, strong, or faithful. *He was chosen because he was available.*

When Simon shouldered the Cross he was undoubtedly met with sneers and boos. Indeed, he was undoubtedly heaped with abuse. Someone in the crowd undoubtedly shouted, "Now you're defiled. Why did you let the Romans trick you." Simon's ears must have tingled with abuse. But I don't think he really minded; for I think the Master must have put a weary arm around him for support, and I think he must have whispered some wonderful words of cheer into Simon's ears!

The night before Jesus had instituted the Lord's Supper. But on this glorious-terrible day he continued a custom that he has never stopped. *The custom is that he always walks with the one who carries a cross.*

Are you weary of your burden? Look at Jesus by your side. He has already carried your cross most of the way. Moreover, the heaviest end is on his shoulder—and this is the end with the roughest edges. And if he isn't carrying it, it is because you won't let him. You must "take your burden to the Lord, and leave it there."

Are you weary of the scorn of the crowd? Look at Jesus. More of the scorn is heaped on him than on you!

Are you weary of your tired, aching, diseased, faltering body? Look at Jesus. He was so weary he fell. And his body was covered with wounds, bruises, spittle, and blood!

When Simon took hold of the Cross, Jesus was so faint he had fallen to the ground. But now that he had Simon to lean on, he gathered a fragment of strength. In the crowd that day there was a large number of women who were weeping and lamenting over Jesus. Presently Jesus spoke to them, "Daughters of Jerusalem, weep not for me, but weep for yourselves, and for your children. For, behold the days are coming, in the which they shall say, Blessed are the barren, and the wombs that never bear, and the paps which never gave suck. Then shall they begin to say to the mountains, Fall on us; and to the hills, Cover us. For if they do these things in a green tree, what shall be done in the dry?" (Luke 23:28-31).

This was a very remarkable prophecy concerning what was to come. We wonder if Jesus would have had the human strength to say these things had it not been for the help of Simon. Perhaps not. Carrying the Cross a short distance may have seemed insignificant to Simon. And yet that act enabled Jesus to preach.

What you are doing for the Master may seem very trivial. But it does enable him to carry on his work. Remember, we are yoke fellows with him. Listen to what Jesus had to say on this matter, "And whosoever shall give to drink unto one of these little ones a cup of cold water only in the name of a disciple, verily I say unto you, he shall in no wise lose his reward" (Matt. 10:42).

That day Simon had to give up taking part in the festivities because he had carried the Cross and thus defiled himself. But whenever we give up something for Christ, we always receive far more in return. Remember Jesus said, "And every one that hath forsaken houses, or brethren, or sisters, or father, or mother, or wife, or children, or lands, for my name's sake, shall receive a hundredfold, and shall inherit everlasting life" (Matt. 19:29).

Simon of Cyrene gave up the Passover week, but in its place he received the "peace that passeth understanding." It was an excellent bargain!

We repeat, Mark tells us that Simon was the father of Alexander and Rufus. But he does not tell us anything about Alexander and Rufus. Why? A reasonable answer may be that it was not necessary. We believe these two sons were well known and loved by the readers of Mark's Gospel in Rome. There is some evidence that they were pillars in the church. Indeed, it is thought by some that Rufus traveled with Peter and Andrew on evangelistic trips. We do know that he was well known to Paul, for at the conclusion of his Epistle to the Romans, he wrote, "Salute Rufus chosen in the Lord, and his mother and mine" (16:13). It seems that the whole family was saved.

But now let us stretch our imaginations to the limit and move the clock ahead some thirty years from the time Simon carried the Cross and go into an obscure part of Rome. Nero has been on the throne since A.D. 54. Because of him, many Christians have been put to death. Peter has been crucified. Paul has been beheaded. Others have been burned to death—some as flaming torches when they were used to light the Circus Maximus so that Nero could race his chariots.

The Christians, however, continued to worship. Let us slip into one of their meetings. A letter of Paul is read; prayer is offered; communion is taken;

a song is sung. Then a leader asks volunteers to rise and tell how they met Christ.

Timothy gets to his feet and tells how he found the Nazarene through the preaching of Paul at Lystra in A.D. 48.

Then John Mark stands up. He tell how he witnessed the arrest of Jesus in the Garden and how he fled home naked. Next, he tells how he found Jesus as his personal Savior and expresses the happiness his Christian life has brought him.

Now Rufus takes the floor. His skin is black. His hair is kinky. His eyes are brown. "I was with my mother and my brother Alexander in the country near Jerusalem," he relates, "when my father went into the Holy City on the fifteenth of Nisan, A.U.C. 784. All of us had planned to go to the Temple that day."

By now every eye is upon him, for the Greeks and the Jews and the Gentiles love this African who worships with them.

"But father didn't come back for a long time, and when he did, I noticed that something remarkable had happened to him. There was a new light in his eyes. His worries and anxieties were gone. But I also noticed large spots of dried blood on his gown, and so I asked him what it was.

"Then he told us the story of the Cross. At first we could not believe that Jesus was actually the Messiah. But we saw the change in father and learned about the Resurrection, and so we knew it was true.

"And that is how our entire family became followers of Jesus Christ!"

Simon of Cyrene bore the Cross patiently. And as a result his rewards were utterly priceless!

s soon to suffer. Then a louder note is heard as
and you saw they are Christ.
the sees Jesus feet and tells many such
affection.   profound

CHAPTER VI

AT THE CROSS

*When Jesus therefore saw his mother, and the
disciple standing by, whom he loved, he saith unto
his mother, Woman, behold thy son! Then saith he
to the disciple, Behold thy mother! And from that
hour that disciple took her into his own home.—*
John 19:26-27.

The cross of Christ, like a skillfully cut diamond,
has many facets. But unlike a diamond, the number
of facets is not limited. If you asked, Does the
Cross have ten thousand facets? The answer would
be: It has ten thousand times ten thousand and
thousands more, and each facet gleams and shim-
mers with divine truth—truth that has transform-
ing power in the hearts of the believers.

One man looks at the Cross, thinks of his sins,
and with a choking voice exclaims:

> *They were nailed to the Cross,*
> *They were nailed to the Cross,*
> *Oh, how much he was willing to bear!*

Another looks at the Cross, thinks of his own un-
worthiness, and with courage flowing from it sings:

> *In the cross of Christ I glory,*
> *Tow'ring o'er the wrecks of time;*

All the light of sacred story
Gathers round its head sublime.

But now let us view a facet seldom seen. Let's go
to the actual spot of crucifixion and watch. This
drama took place on a low hill just outside Jerusalem known as either Calvary or Golgotha.[1] The
spot was easily identified by travelers on either the
Joppa-Jerusalem or Samaria-Jerusalem roads. The
chalk-colored cliffs with their deep eye sockets,
Roman nose, and high forehead, resembled a skull.
The place was a popular landmark.

On that terrible Friday, the fifteenth of Nisan, as
the masses in Jerusalem watched, they could see a
knot of people huddled near the base of those skull-
resembling cliffs. But they paid little attention.
Crosses with screaming victims fastened in place by
ropes or spikes was strictly ho-hum.

The Romans were fond of using terror to enforce
their laws.

Following the slave rebellion led by Spartacus
around 73 B.C., the entire road from the perfume-
city of Capua to Rome was lined with 6000 crosses
with the body of a slave on each. These bodies were
left to rot for many a day in order to impress the
slave population. At the time, when a slave got into
serious trouble, the usual sentence was, *"Pone cru-
cem servo,"* place the cross on the slave.

Standing at the base of the cliff along with the
crowd we notice that the two thieves—tradition
names them Dismas and Cestas—have already
been fastened to their crosses and are now cursing
loudly.

Jesus is still lying on the ground, the crossbeam
on which he is to be nailed is directly beneath his
shoulders. Mary, the mother of Jesus, is standing

[1] Calvary comes from the Latin *calvaria*. The term refers
to a skull. Golgotha is from the Aramaic and has the same
meaning.

nearby. Her face is unusually white—even whiter than the cliffs. And standing by her is John the son of Zebedee. In the Gospels, John usually takes the second place. The usual mention, with only one exception is James and John. But at the Cross he is first.

Suddenly a legionnaire kneels by Jesus. He is a professional executioner and he knows just what to do. With experienced fingers he locates just the place in which to drive the nail. To do this properly required a rudimentary knowledge of anatomy, for the nail had to be so located that it would bear the weight of the body.[2] Then he selected a long, sharp, square-headed nail. He placed the point on the right spot between the bones and raised the hammer.

The sound of the pounding was too much for Mary. She held her hands over her ears, but she could not keep the sound of the hammer or the groans of her eldest son from searing into her brain. Each time the hammer struck the nail she drew in her breath.

But while she shuddered, there were others who rejoiced. After each blow there were sounds of approval from the crowd. "That will teach you to overthrow the Temple money tables," sneers a fat Sadducee as he runs his finger through his long, silky beard.

"And maybe that will teach you not to blaspheme," shouts a slender Pharisee who has always been careful to pay his tithe of anise, mint, and cummin.

The soldier drove the nail home. Then he leaped lightly over the body and hammered the other one into place. Next, after testing the wrists on the crossbeam he signaled for help. With the aid of this

---

[2] For a full discussion of this see, *A Doctor at Calvary* by Pierre Barbet, M.D. Published by Image, a division of Doubleday. Current edition, 1963.

helper the crossbeam was lifted and placed in the mortise of the upright piece, the stipes.

Then he placed one foot of the Galilean on top of the other foot and selected the longest nail he possessed. Next he contemplated about how high the feet should be placed on the stipes. Generally, the higher the feet were placed the longer the victim lived. This was because the high position would allow him to push his body up and thus lessen the strain on his arms and chest.

Having decided on a moderate height for the feet, he placed the nail by their side to ascertain if it was long enough. Satisfied that it was, he pounded it into place.

No one knows whether the cross was the tall or short one.³ But we do know that the sign proclaiming that Jesus was the king of the Jews was tacked into place, probably at the top of the stipes.

The mob had been unhappy with this sign and had approached Pilate. "Write not," said the chief priests, "The King of the Jews; but that he said, I am King of the Jews" (John 19:21).

Having made up his mind, however, Pilate was stubborn. In a short, crisp sentence, he snapped, "What I have written, I have written." (v. 22).

That morning, as the executioner worked, the sky was unusually clear. But at high noon, just after the legionnaire had struck the spike in Jesus' feet for the last time, and had taken his place with the gamblers, a great darkness settled over the earth.⁴

From this point on, for the darkness continued as

---

³ Jim Bishop thinks it was the six-foot one, the *crux humilis*.

⁴ Tertullian, born between A.D. 155 and 160 declared that he had found records of this darkness in the Roman archives. Also, Phlegon stated that in the two hundred and second Olympiad a darkness covered all of Europe. Indeed, he declared that it was so dark the stars could be seen. Thus, it seems, the darkness was worldwide.

Matthew tells us "from the sixth hour . . . unto the ninth hour" (27.:45), the onlookers had to watch closely in order to follow the drama.

Perhaps the purpose of this darkness was to show the world that frequently the greatest blessings come during the darkest periods.

All of Jesus' clothes with the exception of a loin-cloth had been removed. The clothes were then divided among the soldiers, according to custom. But his coat "was without seam, woven from the top throughout. They said therefore among themselves, Let us not rend it, but cast lots for it" (John 19:23-24).

Then one of the men produced some dice and the legionnaires began to gamble for the tunic. They shook the dice in a helmet, and Mary bit her lip. It seemed incredible that men could be so callous while her son was dying and the excruciating pains of hell were gnawing and consuming him.

As she looked into the face of her son, he was twisting in terrible pain. He rolled his head back and forth on the stipes as a man with a high fever rolls his head on his pillow. His teeth chattered in the horrible agony. But mingled with his pathetic groans were the derisive shouts of the mob. "He saved others; let him save himself, if he be Christ, the chosen of God" (Luke 23:35). "Thou that destroyeth the temple, and buildest it in three days, save thyself. If thou be the Son of God, come down from the cross" (Matt. 27:40). "He trusted in God; let him deliver him now, if he will have him: for he said, I am the Son of God" (Matt. (v. 43).

Blood from his feet made a long, irregular line as it followed the grain of the wood and dripped to the chalk-colored earth where it formed a tiny pool. Blood from his hands dripped to the ground like drops in a Roman water clock. But each drop was to Mary like an hour instead of a second.

Each hour seemed an eternity.

As Jesus hung bleeding on the Cross, a thousand things occupied his mind. There was the excruciating pain of the scourging; the pain of the nails in his hands and feet; the pain of the crown of thorns; the pain of his terrible thirst; the pain of infection that was setting in; the pain of the blows he received in his face; the pain of his broken and swollen lips. And in addition to these pains and numerous others, long lines of ants and other insects were undoubtedly tearing at his flesh.

But over and above all of this, there was the terrible pain of heartbreak. Right before his eyes was the city of Jerusalem—the city for which he had wept. And then there was the conspicuous absence of his disciples. Other than John, none was present.[5]

Jesus had called Matthew from the seat of customs. Matthew had prepared a great feast for him and had invited his publican friends to attend. He and Matthew had been extremely close. Jesus had washed Matthew's feet in the Upper Room.

But in this moment of trial Matthew was absent!

Jesus had called Thomas. Thomas had been a faithful follower. When Jesus had decided to go into Judea, Thomas alone urged the disciples to go along by saying, "Let us also go, that we may die with him" John 11:16). Jesus had washed Thomas' feet in the Upper Room.

But in this moment of trial Thomas was absent!

Jesus had loved James, the son of Zebedee. He had promised to make him a fisher of men. James, an impulsive son of thunder had wanted to call fire down on a Samaritan village because the natives had refused hospitality to Jesus. Jesus had washed James' feet in the Upper Room.

But in this moment of trial James was absent!

[5] Luke tells us, "And all his acquaintance, and the women that followed him from Galilee, stood afar off, beholding these things" (23:49). But for practical purposes, they were absent.

All the pains of the Cross, all the pains of ridicule, all the pains of heartache, and all the pains of memory must have scratched their way through the Savior's mind. But John tells us that when he saw his mother, he addressed her.

Mary had a great need. Jesus knew it. And so he focused all his attention on her. She was now approaching fifty—and in those days that was old age. There had been a large family. Besides Jesus, she and Joseph had had four other sons, and at least two daughters.[6]

Jesus and his mother must have been very close. He was the son promised by Gabriel. He was also the oldest and had eaten at her table and grown up in her home. She had held him on her lap, nursed him, hidden him, combed his hair, mended his clothes.

Now, as Jesus looked down on her, he was in great pain. When he allowed his body to sag, the entire weight was on his hands. This bunched the shoulder muscles, tore at the wounds in his hands, and paralyzed the pectoral muscles, making it impossible to exhale.

To get relief from these pains, he could push himself up with his feet. But when he did this, the spike in his feet was like a living flame from hell.

As Jesus hung on the nails, there was acute agony in every muscle, nerve, and portion of his body. But as he spoke to Mary, I think his voice was tender, evenly modulated, and brimming with kindness, hope, cheer—and authority.

Jesus had, of course, to use an economy of words because his life was fast ebbing away. "Woman," he said, 'behold thy son!" (John 19:26).

In every situation Jesus does the best possible thing. This is graphically demonstrated here. As Mary stood beneath him, blinking at her tears she struggled with the wildest emotions a woman could

[6] See Matthew 13:55-56 and Mark 6:3.

know. Any word with a touch of emotion or nostalgia within it might cause her to collapse.

Knowing this, Jesus addressed her with the un-emotional word, *woman*. Then Jesus turned to John and said, "Behold thy mother" (John 19:27). Yes, he used the emotional word with John. But he wanted him to remember that from now on he had a new obligation.

Obligating John to care for his mother was the best possible arrangement Jesus could have made because John's mother Salome was Mary's sister.[*] Jesus' mother would feel at home in her nephew's house. John would make her welcome. Since his conversion, John had continued to grow in love, tenderness, and understanding. And this was just what Mary required.

There is no indication that Mary uttered a single word at the Cross. Yet I believe there is an over-whelming possibility that she might have spoken about as follows:

"Come down, Jesus. You told your disciples in the Garden of Gethsemane that you could summon twelve legions of angels to help you. Summon them now!"

But to this, Jesus was silent.

"Please come down, Jesus. You never did anything wrong in your entire life. Come down and show these people that you are the Son of God!"

But to this, Jesus was silent.

"You raised Lazarus from the grave. You calmed the Sea of Galilee. You fed the multitude with a few loaves. Come down, Son!"

But to this, Jesus was silent.

"Come down; I need you. I'm a widow and you are my eldest son. Oh, Jesus, do—please do—come down!"

But to this, Jesus was silent.

He most certainly could have come down from

[*] Compare Mark 15:40 with Matthew 27:56.

the Cross. It would have been an easy thing to have
done. And had he done so, the Pharisees and the
scribes and the Roman soldiers would have shouted
in one voice,

> He is the Christ ...
> He is the Christ ...
> He is the Christ. ...

But Jesus did not choose to do this. Why? Because of his great love for Mary, and for all mankind. If he had come down from the Cross there
would be no salvation; the power of sin would not
be broken; the grave would still have its victory;
and death would still have its sting!

In stark reality Jesus was not held to the Cross
by nails. No, indeed. He was held to the Cross by
love!

It has frequently been pointed out that Pilate's
sign above the Cross proclaimed Jesus to be the
King of the Jews in Hebrew, Latin, and Greek. And
since Hebrew can be called the language of religion;
Latin the language of law; and Greek the language
of culture, one can also say that Jesus is King in all
these categories. But what is often forgotten is that
when Jesus spoke on the Cross, he spoke in a fourth
language—Aramaic.

The Galilean Aramaic which Jesus used was the
language of the common man: the shopkeeper, the
carpenter, the woman of the streets. It was the language of the man who had never learned Hebrew,
Latin, or Greek.

With this in mind, we can say that Jesus is not
only King to the educated; but that he is also King
to the uneducated. Indeed, to the entire human
race, he is King of Kings and Lord of Lords!

Altogether, Jesus was on the Cross for about
three hours. During this time one of the thieves
"railed on him, saying, If thou be Christ, save thyself and us" (Luke 23:39).

Dismas, the other thief, however was offended by this man's ridicule. Said he, "Dost not thou fear God, seeing thou art in the same condemnation? And we indeed justly; for we receive the due reward of our deeds: but this man hath done nothing amiss" (vs. 40-41).

Then Dismas turned toward Jesus as far as the nails in his hands would allow and, according to the New English Bible, and a number of others, said, "Jesus, remember me when you come to your throne" (Luke 23:42).

This was a most remarkable statement; for in all the Gospels there is no record of anyone else addressing the Lord Jesus Christ with merely a blunt "Jesus." In all other places he is addressed as Teacher, Rabbi, Master, Jesus, thou Son of David, or some other such way.

Because of this "familiarity" on the part of Dismas, some have guessed that perhaps he knew Jesus in his youth. It may be that they went to school together or built a house together. No one knows.

But I think there is a more vital point. And that is that Dismas, seeking mercy, did not go through the customary ritual. And Jesus, most anxious to save him, did not require ritual. He did not say, "You must not be so familiar." Instead, and immediately, he made a solemn promise, "Verily I say unto thee, To-day shalt thou be with me in paradise" (Luke 23:43).

Yes, Jesus is even more anxious to save the lost than water is to flow downhill. But he can save no one unless he asks to be saved!

At the beginning of his ordeal on the Cross, Jesus had prayed, "Father, forgive them; for they know not what they do" (Luke 23:34). But this does not indicate that all people will be saved. For in order to be forgiven, a person must accept the forgiveness. To be valid, a contract has to be accepted by both parties!

Suddenly Jesus cried, "I thirst" (John 19:28). And thirsty he must have been, for he had not had anything to eat or even a single drop of liquid since the Last Supper the night before. This cry was an indication that *his* humanity, like *our* humanity, had its needs—and its limits.

In response to his anguished cry, a soldier soaked a sponge with vinegar and "fixed it on a javelin, and held it up to his lips" (John 19:29, New English Bible).[8]

Jesus drank this vinegar and dropped his head. He was utterly exhausted. But here it should be noted that even before his humanity was about to collapse, his spirit had come to the breaking point. And from his lips the people heard his most pitiful cry, "*Eloi, Eloi, lama sabachthani?* which is, being interpreted, My God, my God, why hast thou forsaken me?" (Mark 15:34).

Could this be another proof that Jesus' spirit was even more vexed than his body? Perhaps!

A moment after he had consumed the vinegar, Jesus said, "Father, into thy hands I commend my spirit" (Luke 23:46). Then he added, "It is finished" (John 19:30).

After this cry, his head slumped and he was dead.

That, however, was not the end of the drama. For the moment he said, "It is finished," ". . . the veil in the temple was rent in twain from the top to the bottom, and the earth did quake, and the rocks rent" (Matt. 27:51).

No one knows what Joseph Caiaphas was doing at this hour, but it is extremely likely that he was in the Temple, for this was the time of the Evening Sacrifice. But whether Caiaphas was there or not there were many priests on duty. And one can

[8] Instead of a javelin, some scholars think the sponge was placed on the end of a stock of hyssop. Père Lagrange, however, thinks that the original Greek word is *hysso*— a short javelin—rather than hyssopo.

imagine their consternation when the extremely heavy veil which Josephus says was sixty feet high was suddenly ripped in two.[9]

This huge veil wonderfully stitched in blue, white, scarlet, and purple was extremely strong. It has been said that two teams of oxen pulling in opposite directions could not rend it. The colors stood for the universe and its four elements. The blue represented the air; the scarlet stood for fire; the white for the earth; and the purple for the sea.

This veil stood in front of Israel's most solemn place—the holy of holies. It was indeed such a solemn place that the high priest alone was allowed to enter it—and he was only allowed to enter it once a year!

But now this veil was utterly ruined, and the fact that it was torn from the top to the bottom was an indication that it was an actual act of God.[10]

To Christians, the destruction of the veil is extremely significant; for it means that the day of a go-between for mankind and God is over—forever. It also means that Christ is now our high priest!

But after Jesus cried, "It is finished" and "gave up the ghost" was he really dead?

Conclusive evidence is that he was. Listen to John, "The Jews therefore, because it was the preparation, that the bodies should not remain on the cross on the sabbath day, (for that sabbath day was an high day,) besought Pilate that their legs might be broken, and that they might be taken

---

[9] Some have said that the lintel which supported the veil was pulverized. This spectacular rent may explain the conversion of so many priests as recorded in Acts 6:7.

[10] It has been stated that an attempt was made to repair the rent, but that the workers finally gave up. This is another indication that all of us have direct access to God. Moreover, the earthly holy place is now gone. The writer of the Book of Hebrews states this fact, "For Christ has entered, not the sanctuary made by men's hands which is only a symbol of the reality, but heaven itself, to appear now before God on our behalf" (9:24, New English Bible).

away. Then came the soldiers, and brake the legs of
the first, and of the other which was crucified with
him. But when they came to Jesus, and saw that he
was dead already, they brake not his legs" (19:31-
33).

The fact that none of Jesus' bones were broken
was a fulfillment of prophecy. John states that
truth in verse 36 like this, "For these things were
done, that the scripture should be fulfilled, A bone
of him shall not be broken."

And yet this is not all the evidence, for even after
the Romans had concluded that he was dead, ". . .
one of the soldiers with a spear pierced his side, and
forthwith came there out blood and water" (v. 34).

In referring to this incident, Doctor Pierre Barbet, M.D., of whom we have made mention earlier,
says, "I say 'wound in the heart' and not wound in
the side, because this has been attested by tradition, and it has been confirmed for me by experi-
ment. The blow of the lance which was given to the
right side reached the right auricle of the heart,
perforating the pericardium."[11]

With this evidence there should be no doubt but
that Jesus was literally, physically dead. Moreover,
we should mention that many dedicated medical
men have studied the evidence; and their general
conclusion is that Jesus Christ died on that solemn
Friday afternoon at approximately three P.M. It
may well be that he died because of a broken heart
rather than because of the nails.

But the fact remains that he died!

All this drama is hard to understand in full. Paul
did not understand it completely. Peter did not understand it completely. Nor can you. But we are
not asked to understand it. We are merely asked to
believe. Understanding is not necessary. Belief is!

The cross of Christ cannot fail to move all of

---

[11] *A Doctor Looks at Calvary.* p. 129. The words were
italicized by Doctor Barbet.

mankind, Christian or not. Mohandas K. Gandhi was born a Hindu and died a Hindu. But when he was asked to name his favorite Christian hymn, he replied immediately that it was, "When I Survey the Wondrous Cross."

Here are those words which meant so much to Gandhi:

> When I survey the wondrous cross
> On which the Prince of glory died,
> My richest gain I count but loss,
> And pour contempt on all my pride.
>
> Forbid it, Lord, that I should boast,
> Save in the death of Christ, my God;
> All the vain things that charm me most,
> I sacrifice them to His blood.
>   —Isaac Watts

CHAPTER VII

NO DEATH

And from that hour that disciple took her unto his own home.—John 19:27.

Easter Sunday has so much meaning that no one who loves the Word should be able to live through the day without a song of supreme joy coming to his lips. Easter is one of God's choice gifts to man.

On Christmas we celebrate the birth of Christ. On Good Friday we celebrate the death of Christ. On Easter we celebrate the Resurrection of Christ. The first Easter celebrated its beginning by replacing unutterable sadness with gladness; tears with laughter; discord with harmony; and doubt with affirmation. The first Easer demonstrated to the world in a most definite and startling way that death is a pause—not a full stop!

Easter is the title page of God's Book of Life, a book of countless pages in which are recorded the names of all who trust in Christ. And traced on that first page are the fadeless words of the Crucified, "whosoever liveth and believeth in me shall never die" (John 11:26).

This wonderful day has a very personal message for everyone who believes in the Lord Jesus Christ. During the last year some of you have had loved ones taken by death. The last scenes of each of these occasions has been sketched forever on and in your minds. You will never forget the last look when you lingered for a long moment and viewed the marble-like features of the departed. Nor will you forget the artificial smile, the cold hands crossed in death, and the carefully pressed suit or dress.

You were then thankful for the flowers. They eased the hurt. But they did not remove it. Likewise, you were thankful for the artificial grass that hid the cruelty of the opened grave. Still, in your imagination you saw the pit that had been dug by unconcerned workmen who labored for so many dollars an hour.

You appreciated the sermon that was preached and the songs that were sung. You were surprised at the sympathy of a host of people—folks you never realized cared so much. That day you discovered you had more friends than you thought.

But ever since, you have been thinking the thoughts that were expressed by Tennyson in "Break, Break, Break":

But O for the touch of a vanished hand,
And the sound of a voice that is still.

It seems that your poor, troubled heart will never be quite the same again, that the wound was much too deep. But if you will only allow it, Easter will put a bubbling new joy in your heart; and you will sing again, laugh again, pray again, plan again— and rejoice again. This is one of the great purposes of Easter.

But it is not the only one!

There are some people who have not lost a loved one for a long time. During the year, the angel of death in his hurry to get his work done passed you by. The shrieking siren was for another. The wreath on the door was for another. The telegram's sad message was for another. But in a very real sense you may have lost something equal to the one who has lost a son, or a wife, or a mother.

Think of the moments of great inspiration we
have had—moments in which we envisioned ourselves accepting Christ, going to college, learning a
trade, working in the church, writing a book, becoming a missionary, or helping a neighbor. But
now these hopes are dead. They have been stran-
gled by the powerful fingers of unseen difficulties,
the snide remarks of friends, the opposition of enemies, or the lack of power to see them through.

The worst of all bankruptcies is the bankruptcy
of enthusiasm!

If this has happened to you, I am glad to tell you
that Jesus Christ and Easter can change your life.

Easter can enable *common* people to do *uncom-
mon* things. Easter can hammer question marks
into exciting exclamation points! Easter can change
corruption into incorruption! Easter can change
failure into success! The Good News of Jesus Christ
delights in taking nothing, adding one, and making
two. Indeed this is the main business of the Gospel![1]

Easter with all its costs, glories, and triumphs, is
meant for you. I mean *you!* There is no reason why
you cannot—even before you finish this book—become a transformed person. But let us go back to
the text at the beginning of the chapter.

That passage tells us that John took Mary, the
mother of Jesus, into his own home. How long she
lingered at the Cross after Jesus had asked John to
care for her we do not know. But I feel certain that
she stayed to the end. One does not have to have
much of an imagination to see what followed after
Jesus had cried, "It is finished." I think Mary must
have remained until Nicodemus and Joseph of Ari-

[1] G od
O ffers
S inful
P eople
E ternal
L ife.

mathea claimed the body. How could anyone have
dragged her away?

Then, it seems to me, that Mary Magdalene,
Mary the mother of Joseph, and Salome must have
gone up to her and said something like this, "You
have gone through enough. You had better return
to the city with John. We will see that the body is
properly placed in the tomb."

One can easily imagine the bereaved mother following John through the twisted and crowded
streets of Jerusalem. Blinded by tears, she needed
someone to show her the way and give her physical
and moral support.

If you are a normal human being, you have had
some sharp disappointments. Perhaps you failed an
important examination, were jilted by one whom
you loved, or suffered a great financial loss. But as
disappointed as you may have been, I can assure
you that no one ever felt the jagged sword of disappointment more keenly than did Mary.

By paging back history some thirty-four years
from the events of Golgotha, we see a slender young
woman in the little Galilean town of Nazereth. Nazareth was a wicked city. Leering soldiers looked
forward to visiting it. Nazareth was wide open.

But in that city there was also that which was
good and kind. Mary was as pure as the carpets of
wild flowers on the hills or the clear water in the
Sea of Galilee. She was a happy girl, for not only
did she have a pure heart but she was also engaged
to a fine young carpenter by the name of Joseph.

Then one fine night the Angel Gabriel came to
her and said, "Hail, thou that art highly favored,
the Lord is with thee; blessed art thou among
women" (Luke 1:28).

This strange address frightened Mary, and so the
angel continued, "Fear not, Mary: for thou hast
found favor with God. And, behold, thou shalt con-
ceive in thy womb, and bring forth a son, and shalt

call his name Jesus. He shall be great, and shall be called the Son of the Highest; and the Lord God shall give unto him the throne of his father David: and he shall reign over the house of Jacob forever; and of his kingdom there shall be no end" (Luke 1:30-33).

Imagine Mary's joy after hearing such an announcement and having it delivered by such a distinguished angel. Her feelings at the time would be impossible to describe. No higher favor had ever been given to a human being—and that favor was given to her!

Having conceived, Mary went to Judea in the south and lived with Elizabeth. And Elizabeth's greeting at the door must have removed any doubt that she might have had in regard to her encounter with Gabriel. Said Elizabeth, "Blessed art thou among women, and blessed is the fruit of thy womb" (Luke 1:42).

The days with Elizabeth were wonderful days—days of planning, rejoicing, and praying. In time her exultation was so great she could not contain the glory of it and remain silent, and so she broke out in what is known today as the Magnificat. Said she:

"My soul doth magnify the Lord, And my spirit hath rejoiced in God my Savior. For he hath regarded the low estate of his handmaiden: for, behold, henceforth all nations shall call me blessed. For he that is mighty hath done to me great things; and holy is his name" (Luke 1:46-49).

In the months that followed, Mary stepped from one joy to another. There was the joy of knowing that the Son of God was developing under her heart. There was the joy of seeing the newborn Child in the straw at Bethlehem. There was the joy of seeing the happiness in the face of the old man Simeon at the Temple. There was the joy of seeing God provide funds for the family to travel to Egypt

and thus escape Herod who was determined to kill
Jesus.[2]

There was the joy of having this loving son grow
up to become Prophet, Priest, and King. And although the other children in the family were skepti-
cal, Mary never doubted.

Never!

Then came the terrible day in which this wonderful son of hers was suddenly arrested, tried, and
condemned. And hours later, as she watched Jesus
suffer and die on the Cross, it seemed to Mary that
all her hopes, dreams and plans had been shredded
into a million pieces.

What a task John had to comfort Mary! What
could he say? He had been by her side as she stared
unbelievingly into the swollen and blood-streaked
face of Jesus. He had felt her shudders at the hammer blows and he had seen the convulsion of her
grief as Jesus raised his voice and with a terrible
cry, groaned, "It is finished," and then became limp
on the Cross.

He knew that he could never erase the picture of
the Cross from Mary's mind. But he had to do
something. What he really did we are not sure. I
like, however, to think that he described to her the
Upper Room experience and then related how
Jesus had said, "Let not your heart be troubled: ye
believe in God, believe also in me. In my Father's
house are many mansions: if it were not so, I would
have told you" (John 14:1-2).

One can imagine Mary rolling and tossing, trying
to sleep. But how impossible it was to doze off when
she realized that her son had died like a felon and
was even then in a tomb.

After the first horrible night I can imagine John
going to her with a new technique—the technique
of remembering her girlhood days. I can visualize

---

[2] It has been thought that the gifts given to Jesus by the
wise men may have been used for this purpose.

him putting an arm around her shoulders and saying gently, "Do you remember the time the Angel Gabriel visited you? Do you remember Elizabeth's greetings at the door and her words of assurance? Do you remember how you were so happy you burst into song and sang, 'My Soul doth magnify the Lord, And my spirit hath rejoiced in God my Savior'?"

Yes, Mary remembered the Magnificat. But how could she ever sing it again? Her son—her perfect son—was dead, and in a shivering tomb! And those nails in Jesus' hands were like nails in her own hands; and the spear in his side was like a spear in her own side. Again and again the scene at Golgotha came before her in bold relief. She could even smell the dust, hear the rattle of the dice, feel the strong arm of John around her, and experience that terrible darkness.

And many things in the house reminded her of him. Over there in the corner were the needles she had used to mend his clothes; and there on the bed was the shawl he had given her. Even her pulse summoned back the sound of hammer blows; and her breath reminded her of those final, searing gasps of Jesus.

Then she remembered the words of Simeon after he had held the infant Jesus in his arms. "This child," he said in his quaking old voice, "is destined to be a sign which men reject; and you too shall be pierced to the heart. Many in Israel will stand or fall because of him, and thus the secret thoughts of many will be laid bare" (Luke 2:34-35, New English Bible).

And now she knew these words were true.

She tried to be brave, but it was hard to be brave.

The long, long minutes of Friday night and all day Saturday and Saturday night were full of anguish. Gloom and despair were everywhere. Even

the birds seemed to have lost their songs and the
wild flowers their beauty.

Often Mary hoped that the whole affair would
turn out to have been a dream. But it wasn't, and
those cold, hard somber facts became more and
more painful the more she thought about them.

It is impossible to piece together all of the information we have about Easter morning unless we
continue to use some imagination—and so we will
do just that.

I think that early that Sunday morning Simon
Peter must have knocked at the door of John in
Jerusalem. (Remember that tradition declares that
John had a branch office in the Holy City from
which he sold fish to the high priest.) Fisherman
Peter, like John, was accustomed to getting up
early. And besides, at this time he'd had a hard
time getting to sleep. There were just too many
things on his mind.

The searing memory of Christ's rebuke in the
Garden; his denial of Christ at the palace of Caia-
phas; and the fact that he hadn't appeared at the
Cross during the crucifixion troubled him.

Indeed, the events of the week were so cata-
strophic it is doubtful if any of the disciples got
much sleep. But this is understandable, for after all
it was the most eventful week in all of human history!

Even before dawn Peter and John were sitting
by the hearth talking about the many things that
had happened. They discussed Mary and her fu-
ture. They talked about plans for the years ahead.
Maybe now that their leader was dead they would
reform their fishing company and go back into the
fishing business. The tranquility of nets and fishing
boats appealed to them.

And then suddenly there was a frantic pounding
at the door. Peter and John exchanged glances.
They knew that Caiaphas had not only hoped to be
rid of Jesus, but also his leading followers. As Peter

looked for a place to hide or a way of escape, John cautiously cracked the door open just wide enough to see; and then recognizing the familiar face of Mary Magdalene, he flung it wide.

"Oh, you must come quickly," she panted, her hand over her heart. "I-I went with these women to the tomb. We had some spices for the body of Jesus. As we walked along, we wondered how we would roll the stone back, for as you know it was quite a large one. But then we got to the tomb, we found that the stone had already been removed.

"Then we went into the tomb and there we saw a young man sitting on the right side. He was clothed in a long white garment³ and we were afraid. And then he began to speak to us. He said, 'You are seeking Jesus of Nazareth who was crucified. He isn't here, for he is risen.' Then after he had shown us the place where the body had been, he added, 'Go tell his disciples and Peter that he is going to Galilee and that they will see him, just as he said.'⁴

"We then left the tomb and began to run over here. That's why I'm so out of breath. On the way we met Jesus! He said, 'All hail.' Then Jesus added, 'Be not afraid: go tell my brethren that they go into Galilee, and there they shall see me' " (Matt. 28:9-10).

By this time, Peter and John were listening so

---

³ Mark speaks of this person as a "young man" (16:5). Matthew speaks of him as an angel whose "countenance was like lightning and his rainment white as snow" (28: 3-4). Luke refers to "two young men (who) stood by them in shining garments" 24:4. John recorded that there were "two angels in white" (20:12).

A study of these statements will show that there is considerable agreement. The angel could have been a young man. Also, all of the writers speak of the clothes as being white. Moreover, each writer was writing from a different point of view.

⁴ These are my own words. See Matthew 28:1-10; Mark 16:1-11; Luke 24:1-9; and John 20:1-8 for this episode.

intently their lips began to form the words that the lips of Mary were forming. Every word, every syllable was extremely important.

"But was the tomb really empty?" asked Peter.

"Yes, it was empty! No one was in it but the shining young man in that dazzling white robe."

John stared vacantly at the women and then at Peter. For a moment he hesitated. Then he leaped out the door and started running toward the garden that belonged to Joseph of Arimathaea—a man the disciples knew well.

As he ran, he could hear the pounding feet of Peter close behind. But just as in their race to the palace of Caiaphas, Peter could not quite keep up.

At the entrance of the tomb, John found that the huge circular stone which had sealed the door had been rolled a short distance away. He stood and looked around, wondering what he should do. But impulsive Peter didn't wait. The moment he came puffing up, his broad shoulders heaving, he lowered his head and strode in. Then he looked around.

The grave clothes had been carefully wrapped and were by themselves in one spot, and the napkin that had been about Jesus' head was in another spot. The tomb was very neat.

Peter told John what he had seen in short, clipped, excited sentences. And then John went in. And to his amazement he found that the tomb was empty just as Peter and the women had said.

It seemed incredible!

Yes, they had seen Lazarus come stumbling out of his tomb after he had been dead four days. And they had seen others raised from the dead. Nevertheless? . . . And yet, still, it had to be true. They began to remember the many times Jesus had spoken about being resurrected on the third day. Slowly Peter counted the days on his fingers, Friday, Saturday, Sunday. Then he looked at John. Their eyes met—and glistened! And then they laughed.

Nevertheless, they wondered.

Peter and John's doubts about the Resurrection were removed at a prayer meeting a short time later. On this occasion the Eleven were present with the exception of Thomas.[5] The doors in the room where they were worshiping were shut. And then, in the midst of their meeting, Jesus suddenly appeared and stood in their midst. He looked deeply into their faces and said, "Peace be unto you" (John 20:19). Following this, he showed them the wounds in his hands and side.

This appearance convinced all who were present. But since Thomas had not been there, he was stubborn. "Except," he said, "I shall see in his hands the print of the nails, and put my finger into the print of the nails, and thrust my hand into his side, I will not believe" (John 20:25).

This was a strong statement for Thomas, for frequently he was one of the first to believe.[6]

Eight days later, the disciples had another prayer meeting. Again the doors were shut. (Perhaps they were afraid of the authorities.) This time all the disciples, including Thomas, were present. And then once again Jesus appeared. As before he repeated his former salutation, "Peace be unto you."

He then went over to Thomas and said, "Reach hither thy finger, and behold my hands; and reach hither thy hand, and thrust it into my side: and be not faithless, but believing" (John 20:27).

Utterly convinced, Thomas answered, "My Lord and my God" (v. 28).

Yes, Jesus had been resurrected. It was a fact. There could be no doubt about it. But Luke knew, perhaps because he was a physician, that there would be those who would cast doubt on the story and say that the body the disciples touched was not the real body or that it was just a spirit. Because of

[5] Judas had committed suicide.
[6] John 11:16.

this, he wrote a very full account of Jesus' return
from death to prove that this body was the actual
resurrected body of Jesus—the very same body
that had been crucified and that had died on the
Cross. Here is part of his account:

"And as they thus spake, Jesus himself stood in
the midst of them, and saith unto them, Peace be
unto you. But they were terrified and affrighted,
and supposed that they had seen a spirit. And he
said unto them, Why are ye troubled? and why do
thoughts arise in your hearts? Behold my hands
and my feet, that it is I myself: handle me, and see;
for a spirit hath not flesh and bones, as ye see me
have. And when he had thus spoken, he showed
them his hands and his feet. And while they yet believed not for joy, and wondered, he said unto
them, Have ye here any meat? And they gave him a
piece of broiled fish, and of a honeycomb. And he
took it, and did eat before them" (Luke 24:36-43).

Before long Mary heard the good news. And immediately she began working with other believers.
Following the crucifixion, she was a broken, troubled woman. Her eyes had been swollen from weeping, her shoulders had drooped in despair. But the
news of Jesus' resurrection changed all of that. It
brought new light to her eyes and a new gleam to
her face. Shoulders straight, step firm, chin erect,
her whole being throbbed and glowed with confidence.

Our last scriptural glimpse of Mary is in the
Upper Room where she had gathered with the
Twelve and other followers to await the Day of
Pentecost.[7] In that crowded room, I think John
must have gone over to speak to her time after
time. And perhaps on one of these occasions, she
may have replied:

"My soul doth magnify the Lord, and my spirit

[7] The number of disciples had been increased again to
twelve by the election of Matthias. Acts 1:23-26.

hath rejoiced in God my Savior. For he hath regarded the low estate of his handmaiden: for, behold, from henceforth all nations shall call me blessed. For he that is mighty hath done to me great things; and holy is his name. And his mercy is on them that fear him from generation to generation" (Luke 1:46-50).

It was her song, and she had a right to repeat it!

To some persons Easter means brightly colored eggs, bunny rabbits, and primp new clothes for the parade. But to the believer, it means immortality, the bringing of life to worthy aspirations, meeting again those who have gone on ahead, living with Christ forever—and having Christ at one's side at all times.

Especially in times of trouble.

John knew that the only way of salvation was through Christ, the Cross, and the Resurrection. Many years after the events in this book, the Apostle John lived in Ephesus where he cared for Mary the mother of Jesus until her death, and was the pastor of the great congregation in that city.

And then, inspired by the Holy Spirit, John began to write the Gospel that bears his name. As his pen sped over the papyrus sheets, his memory was quickened and he remembered with great accuracy.

But John wrote other books as well—and among these are First, Second, and Third John. While writing First John, his mind and soul must have gone back to Golgotha. It was there, with Mary by his side, that he watched Jesus die. And never could he forget the way the crimson blood flowed from Jesus's wounds and slowly dripped, drop by drop, onto the chalk-colored ground. And perhaps remembering this, he wrote, "But if we walk in the light, as he is in the light, we have fellowship one with another, and the blood of Jesus Christ his Son cleanseth us from all sin" (1 John 1:7).

Yes, there is no sin that the blood of Jesus Christ cannot cleanse. But in order that it might be applied to our hearts in that beautiful and mystical way which none of us can completely understand, we must believe!

That's the secret—belief.